AMERICAN LEGAL SYSTEMS:
A RESOURCE AND REFERENCE GUIDE

AMERICAN LEGAL SYSTEMS: A RESOURCE AND REFERENCE GUIDE

Second Edition

Toni Jaeger-Fine
Fordham University School of Law

 LexisNexis®

ISBN: 978-1-4224-2397-4

Library of Congress Cataloging-in-Publication Data

Jaeger-Fine, Toni, author.
American legal systems : a resource and reference guide / Toni Jaeger-Fine, Fordham University School of Law.
pages cm
Includes bibliographical references and index.
ISBN 978-1-4224-2397-4 (softbound)
1. Law—United States. 2. Justice, Administration of—United States. 3. Judicial process—United States. 4. Legal composition. 5. Legal research—United States. I. Title.
KF380.J35 2015
349.73—dc23

2015016711

NOTE TO USERS
To ensure that you are using the latest materials available in this area, please be sure to periodically check the LexisNexis Law School web site for downloadable updates and supplements at www.lexisnexis.com/lawschool.

Editorial Offices
630 Central Ave., New Providence, NJ 07974 (908) 464-6800
201 Mission St., San Francisco, CA 94105-1831 (415) 908-3200
www.lexisnexis.com

MATTHEW◆BENDER

(2015–Pub.3503)

FOR DESIREE

Summary of Contents

Table of Contents

Table of Contents

Table of Contents

Table of Contents

Foreword

It is my hope that this second edition of *American Legal Systems: A Resource and Reference Guide* will be a unique addition to the literature designed to introduce students to the U.S. legal systems. While books on legal research, legal writing, and other introductory matters abound, none presents the fundamentals of the American legal systems in a comprehensive yet accessible way.

That is what *American Legal Systems* strives to do. The book provides an overview of American legal institutions and sources of law, and presents a guide to the interrelationships between and among those institutions and legal authorities. It discusses the defining role of the doctrine of *stare decisis* in the American common law system and the critical judicial review function. In addition, *American Legal Systems* shows the reader how to determine and apply the relative priorities of sources of law, all in the context of the legislative process, agency action, and principles of constitutional and legislative supremacy.

American Legal Systems ties many of these concepts to the realities of law practice. Portions of the book demonstrate how to locate specific resources, use legal terms, and prepare commonplace legal documents.

Among the main virtues of the book is its "reader-friendliness." It introduces readers to some extremely complicated issues of American jurisprudence in a clear and straightforward way. It is relatively short and concise, much of it in chart form, allowing the user to quickly find and assimilate sought-after information. *American Legal Systems* also contains a comprehensive index and extensive internal cross-references, enabling the reader to locate with great ease any term or concept used in the book. As such, *American Legal Systems* could be used for reference purposes in conjunction with a student's substantive course work, or it could be used in connection with an experiential task, such as legal research and writing. Of course, it can also be read on its own.

Given my education and professional experience, I originally conceived *American Legal Systems* for domestic and international law students, but I hope that it will also prove to be a valuable resource for members of the general public and for students of diverse disciplines: government, political science, pre-law studies, paralegal courses, and other areas of instruction. My hope is that *any* student of one or more of these areas will benefit from the foundation in the law presented in this book. While the paradigmatic audience for *American Legal Systems* remains students of law, it should be widely applicable to students in related disciplines.

This version of *American Legal Systems* has reduced the amount of discussion devoted to legal research and related topics given the predominance of fee-based and free computerized research tools.

Toni Jaeger-Fine

New York City

January 2015

Chapter 1

INTRODUCTION TO THE U.S. LEGAL SYSTEMS

This chapter discusses the following:

- The Constitution of the United States of America (A.)
- Sources of U.S. Law and Legal Authorities (B.)
- The U.S. as a Common Law System (C.)
- The Adversarial System of Litigation (D.)

A. THE CONSTITUTION OF THE UNITED STATES OF AMERICA

The Constitution of the United States, ratified in 1790, is the national charter and the highest source of law in the nation. This part addresses the following:

- Component Parts of the Constitution (1.)
- The Articles (2.)
- The Amendments (3.)
- The Structure of the Government Created by the Constitution (4.)

1. Component Parts of the Constitution

Preamble	• Brief introduction to the Constitution • Begins with the familiar words "[w]e the People . . . ." • Not an important textual source — is rarely cited or relied upon by courts or scholars.
Articles	• Overview: ○ Article I — The Legislative Branch ○ Article II — The Executive Branch ○ Article III — The Judicial Branch ○ Article IV — Full Faith and Credit/Privileges and Immunities ○ Article V — The Amendment Process ○ Article VI — Supremacy of Federal Law ○ Article VII — Ratification • See section 2.
Amendments	• 27 Amendments to the Constitution.

	• Two types:
	  ○ Structural changes.
	  ○ Individual rights and liberties.
	• See section 3.

2. The Articles

a. Article I — The Legislative Branch

Establishes U.S. Congress	• Bicameral legislative branch:
	  ○ Senate.
	  ○ House of Representatives.

Legislative Power	• Congress holds "[a]ll [federal] legislative Powers."
	• Lawmaking power exercised by
	  ○ Passing laws by majority vote of each chamber.
	  ○ Overriding a presidential veto by 2/3 vote in both chambers.
	• Limits on congressional power:
	  ○ Powers enumerated in the Constitution.
	  ○ Especially:
	• Article I, section 8.
	• 13th Amendment.
	• 14th Amendment.
	• 15th Amendment.

Other Provisions	• See Chapter 2.A.
	  ○ Representation in each chamber.
	  ○ Terms of office.
	  ○ Qualifications for office.
	  ○ Elections.
	  ○ Special powers of each chamber.

b. Article II — The Executive Branch

Establishes Federal Executive Branch	• Consists of:
	  ○ President
	  ○ Vice President
	  ○ Other, unspecified executive officers. See Chapter 3.

Powers of the President	• Sign or veto legislation passed by Congress. • Execute or administer the laws — the president shall "take care that the laws shall be faithfully executed." • Commander-in-Chief of the military. • Conduct international affairs. • Nominate federal judges, ambassadors, consuls, and other high-level executive officers (subject to "advice and consent" of the Senate).
Representation/ Terms of Office	• Nationwide representation. • 4-year terms. • Limited to two terms.
Qualifications for Office of President	• Natural born citizen. • At least 35 years of age. • At least fourteen years a resident of the U.S.
Elections by Electoral College	• Citizens vote for electors who pledge to cast electoral vote for specific candidate. • Electors chosen within each state by major political parties. • In most states, electoral votes are "all or nothing."

Removal from Office of President, Vice President, Other High Level Executives	• High level executive officers removed from office upon:
	  o Impeachment by majority vote of House of Representatives for "Treason, Bribery, or other high Crimes and Misdemeanors"; and
	  o Conviction by Senate by 2/3 vote.

c.   Article III — The Judicial Branch

Establishes Federal Judiciary	• One Supreme Court. • Other "inferior" courts as established by Congress.

Limits on Federal Judicial Power	• Two primary limits:
	  o Subject matter Jurisdiction.
	  o Justiciability — the "case" or "controversy" requirement.
	• See Chapter 4.A.2.

Selection of Federal Judges	• Nomination by the President; and • Confirmation by the Senate.
Guarantees of Judicial Independence	• No diminution in salary. • Hold office "during good Behaviour" — life tenure absent conviction on impeachment (see immediately below).

Removal from Office	• Federal judges removed from office upon: ○ Impeachment by majority vote of House of Representatives for "Treason, Bribery, of other high Crimes and Misdemeanors"; and ○ Conviction by Senate by 2/3 vote.

d. Article IV — Full Faith and Credit and Privileges and Immunities

Full Faith and Credit	• Each state must give "full faith and credit" to public acts, records, and judicial proceedings of every other state. • Examples: ○ P wins money damages against D in State X. D moves and takes all assets to State Y. P can enforce the judgment of State X in the courts of State Y. ○ H and W marry in State X, although they reside in State Y. State Y recognizes the marriage performed in State X. ■ As of this writing, it is an open question as to whether same-sex marriages must be recognized in states where such marriages are not performed under the clause's public policy exception.
Privileges and Immunities	• "The citizens of each state shall be entitled to all privileges and immunities of citizens in the several states." ○ Protects fundamental rights against efforts to discriminate against out-of-state citizens.

e. Article V — The Amendment Process

State Approval Required	• Requires approval of super-majority of states — cannot be achieved at the federal level alone.
Proposals for Constitutional Amendments	• Proposals for constitutional amendments made by: ○ 2/3 vote of both houses of Congress; or ○ Application of 2/3 of state legislatures.
Ratification	• Ratification of proposed amendments achieved by: ○ 3/4 of the state legislatures; or ○ Conventions in 3/4 of the states.
Difficult to Achieve	• Only 27 amendments in U.S. history. • Popular disinclination to amend the Constitution.

Relevance of the Constitution as a Living Document	• Theory of the "Living Constitution":
	   o Controversial notion of constitutional interpretation.
	   o Constitution should be read as an evolving document that adapts to modern sensibilities.
	   o Gives courts greater flexibility to adapt constitutional interpretation.
	   o Makes formal amendment process somewhat less important.

f. Article VI — Supremacy of Federal Law

Supremacy of Federal Law	• All valid federal law is supreme to and trumps inconsistent state law.

Preemption	• Doctrine derived from and closely related to the doctrine of Supremacy.
	 • Federal law may preempt (preclude) state law in same area when court finds legislative intent to preempt:
	   o Express preemption — state law expressly precluded by words of federal legislation.
	   o Implied preemption:
	     ■ Field preemption:
	       √ Pervasive federal framework.
	       √ Dominant federal interest.
	     ■ Conflict preemption:
	       √ Impossibility preemption — not possible to comply with both federal and state law.
	       √ Obstacle preemption — state law is an obstacle to achieving full congressional goals.

g. Article VII — Ratification

How Achieved	• Ratification of nine of the original states
When Achieved	• 1790

3. The Amendments

The amendments are extremely complex; what follows is a simple statement of the subject(s) of each of the amendments. In order to fully understand the amendments, relevant case law must be consulted.

1st Amendment*	• Right of speech.
	• Right of press.
	• Right of assembly.
	• Religion clauses:
	  ○ Right of free exercise of religion.
	  ○ No establishment of religion.

2nd Amendment*	• Right to bear arms.
3rd Amendment*	• No requirement of quartering soldiers outside of wartime.
4th Amendment*	• Right to be free from "unreasonable searches and seizures."

5th Amendment*	• Prohibition against double jeopardy.
	• Prohibition against compelled self-incrimination.
	• No deprivation of life, liberty, or property "without due process of law."
	• Eminent domain — government may take private property:
	  ○ Only for "public use"; and
	  ○ Must give owner "just compensation."

6th Amendment*	• In criminal trials, rights to:
	  ○ Speedy and public trial.
	  ○ Trial by jury.
	  ○ Be informed of the nature and cause of the accusation.
	  ○ Be confronted with witnesses against defendant.
	  ○ Compulsory process for obtaining witnesses in defendant's favor.
	  ○ Lawyer.

7th Amendment*	• Right to a jury trial in all cases at common law in which the value of the controversy exceeds $20.
8th Amendment*	• Right to reasonable bail. • Right to be free from "cruel and unusual punishment."
9th Amendment*	• Rule of construction that power of federal government may not be extended to unenumerated areas.
10th Amendment*	• Reservation of residual rights to states and people.
11th Amendment	• State sovereign immunity — state immunity from suit absent consent.
12th Amendment	• Election of President and Vice President.
13th Amendment**	• Slavery prohibited.
14th Amendment**	• Due process, applicable to the states. • Equal protection. • Privileges and immunities of citizenship.

15th Amendment**	• Right to vote may not be infringed on the basis of race.
16th Amendment	• Power of Congress to establish income tax.
17th Amendment	• Election of Senators.
18th Amendment	• Prohibition of manufacture, sale, and transportation of alcoholic beverages. • Repealed by 21st Amendment.
19th Amendment	• Women's right to vote.
20th Amendment	• Presidential succession.
21st Amendment	• Repeal of 18th Amendment.
22nd Amendment	• Limits on terms of President.
23rd Amendment	• Presidential vote in D.C.
24th Amendment	• Prohibition of poll or other tax on voting.
25th Amendment	• Presidential succession.
26th Amendment	• Right to vote at age 18.
27th Amendment	• Effective date of changes to congressional compensation.

*   Amendments 1–10 collectively = *Bill of Rights.*
**   Amendments 13–15 collectively = *Reconstruction Amendments.*
Congress given power to enforce these amendments through "appropriate legislation."

4. The Structure of the Government Created by the Constitution

a. Governing Principles of the Constitution

Federalism	• Defines the relationship between the national government and the states. • See section b.
Separation of Powers and Checks and Balances	• Defines the relationship between/among the three branches of the national government. • See section c.

b. Relationship Between State and Federal Governments: Federalism

Federalism Defined	• A power sharing arrangement between the national/federal government and the states. • *Vertical* separation of powers.

Limited Powers of the Federal Government	• The federal government's powers are limited: 　○ National government's powers are limited to those that are enumerated in the Constitution. 　○ No general police power = power to legislate in areas that the national government thinks would be in the best interests of the general public.
States Hold Remaining Governmental Power	• The states retain residual governmental powers. • State governments: 　○ Are the product of state constitution and laws. 　○ Consist of: 　　■ Legislative branch — often bicameral, like the federal government. 　　■ Executive branch — headed by a governor. 　　■ Judicial branch — typically consisting of trial level courts, intermediate appellate courts, and courts of last resort. See Chapter 4.A.3.
Principal Powers of the Federal Government	• Primary Sources: 　○ Article I section 8 grants numerous powers, including the following: 　　■ Tax and spend. 　　■ Immigration/naturalization. 　　■ Bankruptcy. 　　■ Weights and measures. 　　■ Currency. 　　■ Copyrights and patents. 　　■ Establish and empower federal courts. 　　■ Declare war. 　　■ Ratify treaties. 　　■ Interstate and international commerce (see immediately below). 　○ 13th Amendment — power to enforce prohibition on slavery. 　○ 14th Amendment — power to enforce due process and equal protection guarantees, *inter alia*. 　○ 15th Amendment — power to enforce prohibition on voting discrimination.
Special Note on the Federal Power over Interstate Commerce	• Congress's power to regulate "commerce among the several States" includes power over: 　○ Channels of interstate commerce; 　○ Instrumentalities of and persons or things in interstate commerce; and 　○ Activities having a substantial relation to/that substantially affect interstate commerce — broad range of activities that include the following: 　　■ Banking. 　　■ Antitrust/competition law.

	▪ Securities regulation. ▪ Federal financial crime. ▪ Trademarks. ▪ Labor law. ▪ Product safety.

Primary Powers of the States	• Include the following:
	  ○ Family law.
	  ○ Criminal law.
	  ○ Law of real property.
	  ○ Contract law.
	  ○ Corporate law.
	  ○ Tort law.
	  ○ Employment law.
	  ○ Trust and estate law.
	  ○ Education law.
	• State substantive and procedural laws vary — sometimes significantly — from state to state.

c. Relationship Between and Among Branches of National Government: Separation of Powers and Checks and Balances

In General	• Define the relationship between and among the three branches of the federal government. • Based on fear of centralized government.

Separation of Powers	• Each branch of the national government has its own defined functions:
	  ○ Legislative branch — makes federal law.
	  ○ Executive branch — executes federal law.
	  ○ Judicial branch — interprets and applies the law.
	• *Horizontal* separation of powers.

Checks and Balances	• Each branch has some control or "check" over each of the other branches.
	• Examples:
	  ○ Legislative controls over executive branch:
	    ▪ Control over budget.
	    ▪ Power to override presidential vetoes.
	  ○ Legislative controls over judicial branch:
	    ▪ Control over budget.
	    ▪ Control over court structure and jurisdiction.
	  ○ Executive controls over legislative branch:
	    ▪ Power to veto legislation.
	    ▪ Power to enforce legislation.
	  ○ Executive controls over judicial branch:

<table>
<tr><td></td><td>

    ■ Power to nominate federal judges.
  ○ Judicial controls over legislative branch:
    ■ Power to review and declare unconstitutional acts of Congress.
  ○ Judicial controls over executive branch:
    ■ Power to review and declare unconstitutional actions of the President.
    ■ Power to review and declare agency action to be unconstitutional or inconsistent with federal legislation.
</td></tr>
</table>

B.   SOURCES OF U.S. LAW AND LEGAL AUTHORITIES

This part covers the following:

- Introduction (1.)
- Primary Versus Secondary Authorities (2.)
- Secondary Authorities (3.)
- Legal Authorities as Binding or Persuasive (4.)
- Hierarchy of Sources of Law (5.)
- Case Reporters and Digests (6.)

1.   Introduction

Types of Legal Authorities	• Primary:
	  ○ Impose binding rights and obligations.
	  ○ The "law."
	• Secondary:
	  ○ Do not impose binding rights or obligations.
	  ○ Not "the law."

Binding Nature of Legal Authorities	• Mandatory/binding/controlling authorities:
	  ○ Must be followed by court when applicable.
	  ○ Primary sources only.
	• Persuasive authorities:
	  ○ Should be consulted in the absence of relevant binding authority.
	  ○ May be followed or not, depending on whether it persuades the judge that it is correct.
	  ○ May include primary and secondary authorities.

2.   Primary Versus Secondary Authorities

Primary Authorities	• Authorities that create binding rights and obligations.
	 • Examples:
	    ○ Constitutions (federal and state).
	    ○ Statutes/legislation (federal and state).
	    ○ Administrative rules and regulations and other executive issuances (federal and state).
	    ○ Case law (federal and state).

Secondary Authorities	• Authorities that do not create binding rights and obligations but that describe, summarize, criticize, seek change to, or otherwise discuss the law. • See examples discussed in the chart immediately following.

3.   Secondary Authorities

Treatises	• Specific treatment of multitude of issues in a particular area of law. • Multi-volume. • Provide detailed information about a particular area of law. • Updated frequently. • Certain well-known scholars carry significant prestige with courts in their respective area of expertise.
Restatements	• State *and* analyze common law principles on national basis; show trends, make recommendations. • Joint effort by panels of noted specialists in area. • Deal with various substantive topics, often focusing on state approaches. • Appendix volumes contain case digests and citations. • Given considerable respect by courts. • Respectable source of secondary authority.
Law Review/Law Journal Articles	• Scholarly writings on discrete, fairly specific areas of law. • Most are student edited. • Articles authored by professors and students, and sometimes judges or practitioners. • Journals may be general or specific (by theme/area of law). • Primarily of scholarly interest — often criticized for not being useful to practitioners and judges.

American Law Reports (A.L.R.)	• Two components:
	  ○ Cases — limited number of cases "reported" [Note: never use the A.L.R. "citation"].
	  ○ Annotations — discussion of reported case and related cases; detailed discussions along lines of narrow topic.
	• Various sets: A.L.R. Fed; A.L.R.1st; A.L.R.2d; etc.
	  ○ Federal cases are reprinted and annotated in A.L.R.1st and A.L.R.2d through 1969.
	  ○ Since 1969, (select) federal cases are reprinted and annotated in A.L.R. Fed.
	• Topics unsystematic — many important topics not addressed at all.
	• Little authoritative value — do not quote from or cite.

Hornbooks	• Very general, background information. • Not comprehensive. • Very concise and clear. • Useful if you have no familiarity with a topic. • Generally do not carry much weight with courts.
Legal Encyclopedias	• Several types, including American Jurisprudence (Am. Jur.) and Corpus Jurus Secundum (C.J.S.). • Organized topically by legal issue/subject. • Gives overview and guides user to primary authority and other resources. • Case-finding tool — leads to cases in many jurisdictions. • Good place to begin when you know little or nothing about the subject. • Very little authoritative value — do not cite.
Commercial Looseleaf Services	• Specialized and administrative fields. • Organized by area of law — often by agency or other responsible government entity.
Practice Guides	• Most common for litigation practice and procedure. • Useful practice guides include those that detail various court rules and statutory provisions relating to judicial organization and practice.
Form Books	• Organized by area of law and jurisdiction. • Judicious use of form books can save time and money. • Use should always be accompanied by careful evaluation and modification as may be necessary.

Internet	• A multitude of Internet sites — use caution as there are many non-reputable sites.
	  ○ .gov sites generally reputable.
	  ○ .com and .net sites vary enormously.

4. Legal Authorities as Binding or Persuasive

Binding/Mandatory/ Controlling	• Must be followed by a court when applicable.
	• Only primary legal sources may be binding.
	• Examples:
	  ○ Relevant constitutional provisions (federal and state)
	  ○ Relevant statutory/legislative provisions (federal and state)
	  ○ Relevant administrative issuances (federal and state)
	  ○ Some case law; which cases are binding is determined by a number of factors. See Chapter 4.B.3.

Persuasive	• Authorities that are not binding but that a court should consult in the absence of mandatory authority.
	• Court is free to follow or reject legal principles announced in persuasive authority.
	• Examples:
	  ○ Non-binding case law.
	  ○ Secondary authorities.

5. Hierarchy of Sources of Law

Federal Law Versus State Law	• Valid federal law is always supreme to state law.
Priority within Sovereignties	• Constitution. • Statutes/legislation. • Agency rules and regulations/other executive issuances. • Case law. ○ Note: Although case law falls fairly low on the priority of sources of law, this is misleading. Relevant case law must *always* be considered when dealing with a constitutional, statutory, or administrative provision; as explored below in greater detail, there is no meaningful way to interpret or apply other primary sources of law without reference to relevant, binding case law.
Secondary Sources	• May be consulted in absence of controlling primary sources. • Use secondary sources that have greater authority/ credibility. • See Part B.3.

6. Case Reporters and Digests

Case Reporters	• Volumes that contain reported cases. • Organized by jurisdiction and hierarchy.
Case Digests	• Case finding tools organized around subject/topic indices. • Provide blurbs about cases and citation to case reporters.
See Also	• Chapter 4.B.2.

C. THE U.S. AS A COMMON LAW SYSTEM

Hallmarks of Common Law System	• Relies heavily on court precedent in subsequent adjudications.
Defining Role of Doctrine of *Stare Decisis*	• *Stare decisis* = "let it stand." • Tendency of U.S. courts to follow principles of law announced in earlier judicial opinions when presented with similar facts.
Types of Precedent	• Precedent based on constitutional provisions. • Precedent based on legislative/regulatory provisions. • Pure decisional law.

Binding Versus Persuasive Nature of Precedent	• Binding/controlling/mandatory:
	  ○ Must be followed and applied by judge in subsequent cases unless the facts of the precedent can be distinguished on a principled basis.
	• Persuasive:
	  ○ Authority that a court considers in the absence of binding precedent.
	  ○ Court may follow or not persuasive precedent.
	• Which precedent is binding and which is persuasive?
	  ○ Whether precedent is binding or persuasive depends largely on the issuing court(s) and the relationship of the issuing court(s) and the court before which the case is currently pending. See Chapter 4.B.3.

Versus Civil Law Systems	• Some attributes of civil law systems:
	  ○ Common in many other countries in the world.
	  ○ Civil law systems rely heavily on statutory codes, which are interpreted broadly to answer virtually any legal issue.
	  ○ Civil law courts consider precedent but rarely are bound by decisions of earlier courts:
	    ▪ Generally no requirement that court explain why precedent not followed.

	• Some civil law countries have limited rules for the binding nature of precedent.
See Also	• Chapter 4.

D.   THE ADVERSARIAL SYSTEM OF LITIGATION

Attributes	• Relies on attorneys representing the position of the client before an impartial decision-maker: ○ Effective adversarial representation critical to success.
Role of Trial Judge	• Relatively passive. • Generally only responds to requests by parties and does not make rulings *sua sponte* (on its own motion): ○ Important exception in cases where court has doubt about its authority to decide the case.
Fact Discovery	• Parties responsible for extensive process of pre-trial fact discovery. • Judge is largely absent from the process of fact discovery. • See Chapter 5.B.2.
Limits on Appeals	• Appeals limited to: ○ Issues of law — findings of fact generally cannot be reviewed. ○ Record created below — no new evidence may be received by the court of appeals. ○ Issues preserved — the appellate court may not review issues not raised and properly preserved below.

Chapter 2

STATUTORY LAW AND LEGISLATIVE HISTORY

This chapter covers the following:

- U.S. Congress: A Bicameral Institution (A.)
- Terminology Relating to Congressional Action (B.)
- How Laws are Passed (C.)
- Sources of Federal Statutory Law (D.)
- Statutory Interpretation (E.)
- Finding Legislative History of a Federal Statute (F.)

A. U.S. CONGRESS: A BICAMERAL INSTITUTION

The U.S. Congress is a bicameral institution consisting of:

- The U.S. House of Representatives (1.); and
- The U.S. Senate (2.)

1. The U.S. House of Representatives

The "Lower" Chamber	• Known as the lower chamber despite fact that it has same lawmaking power as the Senate.
Number of Members	• 435, divided among states proportional to population.
Qualifications for Office	• At least 25 years of age. • At least 7 years a citizen of the U.S. • Inhabitant of state from which chosen.
Terms of Office	• 2-year terms. • Unlimited re-election possible.
Elections	• Direct elections within congressional districts, drawn within states. • Members represent people in their congressional district.
Special Powers	• Spending legislation must begin in House. • Power to impeach federal judges and high-level executive officials.

2. The U.S. Senate

The "Higher" Chamber	• Known as the higher chamber despite fact that it has same lawmaking power as the House.
Number of Members	• 100. • 2 per state.
Qualifications for Office	• At least 35 years of age. • At least 9 years a citizen of the U.S. • Inhabitant of state from which chosen.
Terms of Office	• 6-year terms. • Unlimited re-election possible.
Elections	• Direct statewide elections.
Special Powers	• Ratifies treaties. • Confirms major presidential appointees, including department heads, ambassadors and consuls, and federal judges. • Tries impeached officials.

B. TERMINOLOGY RELATING TO CONGRESSIONAL ACTION

Congressional action has a language all its own. Set forth below is terminology peculiar to the legislative process and the meaning of those terms.

Amendment	• Addition to bill or resolution; may be made at any time after introduction; often made to help forge compromise.
Bill	• Proposed legislation introduced into either or both houses of Congress.
Chamber	• Each "house" of Congress may also be referred to as a "chamber."
Codification	• Process of adding laws into a code (for example, the United States Code, see Chapter 2.D.).
Enabling Statutes	• Statute that creates and empowers ("enables") an administrative agency to act. Also called "implementing" statute.
Public Law	• Chronological assignment of number to each law. • Assigned when President signs a bill or when a presidential veto is overridden. • Number comprised of year of congress and chronological number of bill, separated by hyphen.
Resolution	• Congressional expression of opinion, thanks, censure, among other things. • Not a law.
Rider	• Specific type of amendment that has little or no connection to the substance of the bill.

	• Generally attached to bill or resolution with the specific purpose of coercing opponents to favor passage of the bill or resolution.
Session Laws	• Chronological compilation of all laws enacted by a legislature in a particular legislative session. • Found in Statutes-at-Large. • Legal evidence of laws, many of which have been codified. • Not useful as research tool except insofar as a particular law has not yet been published in the U.S.C.
Slip Laws	• First official form of publication of a federal law. • Separately paginated pamphlet containing text of each law. • Designated by public law number.

C. HOW LAWS ARE PASSED

Introduction of a Bill	• Bill = proposed law. • Introduced one or more members — sponsors — into their respective chambers. • Same or similar versions of the same bill may be introduced in both chambers at the same time.
Committee/ Subcommittee Assignment	• Each chamber has committees, and each committee has a range of sub-committees. • Each bill assigned to a relevant committee for consideration. • Committee assigns bill to relevant subcommittee for consideration. • All committees and subcommittees chaired by members of majority party in that chamber.
Subcommittee Hearings and Reports	• Testimony by agencies, corporations, interest groups, individuals, organizations, etc. • Subcommittee issues report on pending bills for consideration by full committee and/or full chamber. • Subcommittee may revise language of bill. • Subcommittee may advance bill to full committee or may essentially kill bill by not reporting it to full committee.
Committee Hearings and Reports	• Testimony by agencies, corporations, interest groups, individuals, organizations, etc. • Committee issues report on pending bills for consideration by full chamber. • Committee may revise language of bill.

	• Committee may advance bill to floor of chamber or may essentially kill bill by not reporting it to the full chamber.
Floor Debates and Reports	• Floor debates on bill in each chamber. • Members may prepare and submit written statements in support of, or opposition to a bill. • Chamber may revise language of bill. • Filibuster = dilatory tactic in the Senate that can be used to delay vote on a particular measure.
Chamber Votes	• Each chamber votes on bill. • Simple majority of each chamber required to pass bill.
Joint Conference	• Bill passed by both chambers must be identical.

Reports (if necessary)	• Joint Committee:
	  ○ Convened to resolve differences between House and Senate version of a bill.
	  ○ Comprised of members of both chambers.
	• Report of Joint Committee explains joint bill, which then goes to each chamber for passage.

Presentation of Bill to President	• President may:
	  ○ Sign the bill into law and may issue signing statement.
	  ○ Veto bill and issue veto statement (see below *re* override of presidential veto).
	  ○ Do nothing — bill will become law after 10 days unless Congress has adjourned (pocket veto).

Overriding Presidential Veto (if necessary)	• Two-third of each chamber required to override presidential veto.

D. SOURCES OF FEDERAL STATUTORY LAW

United States Code (U.S.C.)	• Contents:
	  ○ Text of statutes.
	  ○ Legislative annotations.
	• Published by Congressional Printing Office.
	• Official version — always cite to this official version when available.
	• How to locate material:
	  ○ Index, by subject, name of act, and popular name.
	  ○ Title outline — 54 titles divided into chapters and subchapters.

United States Code Annotated (U.S.C.A.)	• Contents:
	  ○ Text of statutes.
	  ○ Legislative annotations.

	○ Notes of Decisions — case annotations for each statutory provision, with index.
	○ References to C.J.S. and other West resources.
	• Published by West.
	• How to locate material:
	○ Index, by subject, name of act, and popular name.
	○ Title outline — 54 titles divided into chapters and subchapters.
	• Use for research purposes only; never cite to or quote.
United States Code Service (U.S.C.S.)	• Contents:
	○ Text of statutes.
	○ Legislative annotations.
	○ Interpretive Notes and Decisions — case annotations for each statutory provision, with index.
	○ References to A.L.R. and other Lexis resources.
	• Published by LexisNexis.
	• How to locate material:
	○ Index, by subject, name of act, and popular name.
	○ Title outline — 54 titles divided into chapters and subchapters.
	• Use for research purposes only; never cite to or quote.
United States Code Congressional and Administrative News (U.S.C.C.A.N.)	• Content:
	○ Public laws from each congressional session.
	○ Major congressional committee and sub-committee reports.
	○ No annotations.
	• Organized chronologically.
	• Locate by Public Law number.
Statutes at Large	• Compendium of enacted laws and resolutions that constitute official proof of enactment.
	• Organized chronologically by public law number.
Session Laws	• Compilation of slip laws from immediately preceding congressional session.
	• Organized chronologically by public law number.
Slip Laws	• Individual law in pamphlet form.
	• Organized chronologically by public law number.

E. STATUTORY INTERPRETATION

The following tools of construction can be used to determine the meaning of a statute. Remember to always consult relevant case law when attempting to interpret a statutory provision.

Plain Meaning Rule	• The language of a statute is the starting point for analysis.
	  ○ Ordinary and Specialized Meanings:
	    ■ Words are generally given their ordinary meaning.
	    ■ Terms of art defined in statute are given that meaning.
	    ■ Accepted industry meaning is given that meaning.
	• When plain meaning rule does not produce a clear result, the tools of interpretation listed below may be used.

Tools That Look at Relationship Among Words of Statute	• General, specific, and associated words:
	  ○ Specific terms override general terms.
	  ○ *Noscitur a sociis* — words grouped in a list should be given a related meaning.
	  ○ *Ejusdem generis* — where general words follow an enumeration of persons or things, such words are construed as applying only to persons/things of the same general kind or class as those specifically mentioned.
	  ○ *Expressio unius est exclusio alterius* — when one or more things of a class are expressly mentioned, others of the same class are understood to be excluded.
	• The effect of statutes *in pari materia*:
	  ○ Statutes *in pari materia* are those that pertain to the same subject matter.
	  ○ Statutes *in pari materia* should be interpreted in light of each other.
	• Grammatical rules and punctuation:
	  ○ May clarify statutory meaning, but courts typically do not place primary meaning on such elements.
	• Statutory language not to be construed as surplusage:
	  ○ Court should give effect to every clause and word of a statute and should read legislation to avoid rendering any statutory language superfluous.
	• Same phrasing in same or related statutes:
	  ○ A term is generally given the same meaning every time it appears in a statute.
	• Congress knows how to say . . . :
	  ○ Congress knows how to say things that are expressly provided for elsewhere.
	  ○ Failure to do so generally suggests that Congress intended something different.
	• Titles of acts or sections/preambles:

	○ The title of an act or section/statutory preamble can aid in resolving an ambiguity in the text, but it may not enlarge or confer powers. • Findings and purposes sections: ○ Courts may look to legislative findings and purposes to help clarify congressional intent. • Severability: ○ Severability = ability of rest of statute to remain in effect upon finding of unconstitutionality of some portion(s) of the statute. ○ General presumption in favor of severability. ○ Presumption reinforced by a severability provision in the legislation.
Tools That Look at Relationship Between Words of a Statute and External Material	• Legislative acquiescence: ○ Strong authoritative effect of judicial opinions that the legislature has acquiesced in by lapse of time without action. • Timing of legislation: ○ The latest in time prevails when statutes are in conflict. • Departure from common law/established interpretation: ○ Presumption in favor of continuing common law. ○ Courts generally expect that Congress will explicitly so state if it intends a departure from judge-made law. • Avoidance of constitutional issues: ○ Courts avoid constitutional issues when possible. ○ Courts tend to construe statutes, whenever possible, to avoid a finding of unconstitutionality. • Extraterritorial application disfavored: ○ Absent compelling evidence to the contrary, courts construe legislation to apply only within the United States. • Pre-enactment legislative history: ○ Use of pre-enactment legislative history (such as committee/sub-committee reports, sponsor remarks, amendments, committee hearings) is highly controversial. ○ Many believe that prudent use of pre-enactment legislative history can help illuminate congressional intent. ○ Others believe that use of legislative history is opportunistic and even violates separation of powers: ■ Theory = Congress speaks only through the words of an enacted law.

	• Post-enactment or subsequent "legislative history": ○ Subsequent legislation may be used by a court to help determine legislative intent. ○ Reenactment of a statute with no change to a provision that has been the subject of an administrative or judicial interpretation is generally seen as a ratification of/acquiescence in that interpretation.

F. FINDING LEGISLATIVE HISTORY OF A FEDERAL STATUTE

The chart below describes the different publications and the legislative history events found in each of those publications. For a discussion of the use of legislative history in statutory interpretation, see Part E.

Congressional Record	• Contents: ○ Introduction of bills and resolutions. ○ Text of some of the more important bills in original or amended form. ○ Text of floor debates. ○ Official voting record and vote tallies. • Published daily while Congress in session. • "Daily Digest" section includes summary of action in each house, dates of committee hearings, bills signed, committee hearings scheduled for the following day. • "History of Bills and Resolutions" index published every two weeks. • Cumulative Index.
Statutes-at-Large	• Compilation of federal session laws, ordered by public law number. • Index for acts contained in that volume only. • References to Congressional Record.
CCH Congressional Index	• Digest of all public bills and resolutions. • Status table reports action on bills and resolutions. • Updated weekly while Congress is in session. • Reports status of all pending legislation. • Lists committee referrals. • Records votes and indicates members who did not vote with the majority of their party. • Measures enacted are indexed by public law number, bill number, sponsor, and subject.

United States Code Congressional and Administrative News (U.S.C.C.A.N.)	• Text of public laws. • Text of selected committee reports. • Major legislative reports with related public law and some other relevant publications after passage of a law. • Quick reference to legislative history — located before text of each act, cross-reference to page on which legislative history appears. • References to House and Senate reports.
CIS Abstract/Index	• Abstracts and indexes documents comprising legislative history of statutes. • Compilation of complete legislative history for every public law during each year. • Includes hearing transcripts, reports, committee prints, references to Congressional Record, member voting records, and status records. • Two volumes for each Congress; monthly supplements; quarterly and annual cumulative index. • Index of all bills introduced, by testimony, subject, sub-committee, title, bill number, report number, and document numbers.
Digest of Public General Bills and Resolutions	• Summaries of all bills and resolutions introduced in each session. • Indices by sponsor and cosponsor, short title, and subject.
Monthly Catalog of U.S. Government Publications	• Listing of and index to government publications.

Chapter 3

ADMINISTRATIVE AND OTHER EXECUTIVE LAW

This chapter covers the following:

- Preliminary Points Relating to Agencies and Federal Administrative Law (A.)
- Agency Actions and Issuances (B.)
- The Code of Federal Regulations (C.)
- The Federal Register (D.)
- Presidential Documents (E.)

A. PRELIMINARY POINTS RELATING TO AGENCIES AND FEDERAL ADMINISTRATIVE LAW

Agencies as Creatures of Congress	• Congress establishes federal agencies through authorizing/enabling/implementing legislation. • Congress often provides only vague details or outlines, and agency provides detail by promulgating rules pursuant to the power delegated to them by Congress.
Part of Executive Branch	• Agencies administer federal law. • Form part of executive branch.
Areas of Regulation	• Federal agencies regulate a wide swath of issues as exemplified by the list of agencies below. • Individual states have agencies dealing with the range of issues subject to state law.
Authorizing/ Implementing/ Enabling Legislation	• Legislation that establishes and empowers particular agencies. • Provides specific rules of procedure for the relevant agency that supplement Administrative Procedure Act requirements (see below).

Administrative Procedure Act (APA)	• Statute that governs procedures by which federal agencies propose and establish rules:
	  ○ Includes provisions for public notice and comment, among other things.
	  ○ Contains provisions for judicial review of agency action.
	• Supplemented by requirements in enabling legislation.

Legislative and Judicial Activities	• Agencies engage in both quasi-legislative and quasi-judicial activities.
	• Quasi-legislative role:
	  ○ Rulemaking pursuant to APA.
	• Quasi-adjudicative role:
	  ○ Trial-type hearings held by Administrative Law Judge (ALJ).
	  ○ ALJ makes initial merits disposition.
	  ○ Internal appeal permitted to full board or agency:
	    ■ Rehearing of agency decision may be required by statute.

Court Challenges to Agency Action	• Right to appeal final agency action to federal district court or court of appeals, depending on implementing legislation.
	• Appeal may be taken of:
	  ○ Final agency rules; or
	  ○ Final agency decision in adjudication.
	• Bases for appeal:
	  ○ Agency action was arbitrary and capricious or otherwise contrary to law.
	  ○ Agency action did not follow procedural requirements.
	  ○ Agency action went beyond its congressional mandate.

Major Federal Departments, Agencies, and Commissions	• Agency for International Development. • Bureau of Alcohol, Tobacco & Firearms. • Bureau of Engraving and Printing. • Central Intelligence Agency. • Consumer Product Safety Commission. • Defense Intelligence Agency. • Department of Agriculture. • Department of Commerce. • Department of Defense. • Department of Education. • Department of Energy. • Department of Health and Human Services. • Department of Homeland Security. • Department of Housing & Urban Development. • Department of the Interior. • Department of Justice. • Department of Labor. • Department of State. • Department of Transportation. • Department of the Treasury. • Department of Veterans Affairs.

	<ul><li>Drug Enforcement Administration.</li><li>Environmental Protection Agency.</li><li>Equal Employment Opportunity Commission.</li><li>Federal Aviation Administration.</li><li>Federal Bureau of Investigation.</li><li>Federal Communications Commission.</li><li>Federal Deposit Insurance Corporation.</li><li>Federal Election Commission.</li><li>Federal Emergency Management Agency.</li><li>Federal Energy Regulatory Commission.</li><li>Federal Reserve System.</li><li>Federal Trade Commission.</li><li>Food & Drug Administration.</li><li>General Services Administration.</li><li>Government Accountability Office.</li><li>Government Printing Office.</li><li>Immigration and Naturalization Services.</li><li>Internal Revenue Service.</li><li>International Monetary Fund.</li><li>National Aeronautics & Space Administration.</li><li>National Archives & Records Administration.</li><li>National Endowment for the Arts.</li><li>National Endowment for the Humanities.</li><li>National Highway Traffic Safety Administration.</li><li>National Institutes of Health.</li><li>National Labor Relations Board.</li><li>National Transportation Safety Board.</li><li>Nuclear Regulatory Commission.</li><li>Occupational Safety and Health Administration.</li><li>Office of Personnel Management.</li><li>Peace Corps.</li><li>Securities & Exchange Commission.</li><li>Small Business Administration.</li><li>Social Security Administration.</li><li>U.S. Postal Service.</li></ul>

B.   AGENCY ACTIONS AND ISSUANCES

The following chart depicts various agency issuances and the characteristics and purposes of each of those issuances.

It is of course imperative when doing research in the area of administrative law that case law (in particular federal cases when researching a matter of federal regulatory law) involving the relevant statutory scheme be consulted in addition to agency issuances.

Adjudications	• Agency acting in its quasi-judicial role. • Resolution of disputes between parties. • Normally reviewed in the first instance by Administrative Law Judge (ALJ), with appeal to full agency. • Sources: Federal Register and daily issuances of agency.
Interpretive Guidelines/ Regulation Preambles	• Agency statements explaining and clarifying newly promulgated rules. • Generally entitled to less weight than regulations themselves. • Sources: Code of Federal Regulations, Federal Register, and daily issuances of agency.
Notices	• Designed to put interested persons on notice of a filing by a regulated entity or action by agency. • Sources: Federal Register and daily issuances of agency.
Notices of Inquiry (NOI)	• Precursor to Notice of Proposed Rulemaking (see below). • Agency's initial, tentative thinking re instituting a rulemaking on a specific subject. • Calls for public comment. • Sources: Federal Register and daily issuances of agency.
Notices of Proposed Rulemaking (NOPR)	• Agency notice that it is considering a rulemaking on a specific subject. • Calls for public comment. • Sources: Federal Register and daily issuances of agency.
Opinions	• Administrative Law Judge's determination based on factual findings applied to the law. • Can be appealed to the full board or agency. • Sources: Federal Register and daily issuances of agency.
Orders	• Final disposition of an agency proceeding other than a rulemaking. • Sources: Federal Register and daily issuances of agency.
Policy Statements	• Statements of agency expectation as to how it will rule in a given area or on a specific issue. • Non-binding and therefore not subject to judicial review. • Sources: Federal Register and daily issuances of agency.

Rehearing/ Reconsideration	• Agency re-evaluation of its earlier action at the request of one or more parties. • Requirement of rehearing or reconsideration varies by agency. • If required, must be undertaken as a pre-requisite to judicial review. • Sources: Federal Register and daily issuances of agency.
Rules and Regulations	• Agency issuances of general applicability. • Sources: Code of Federal Regulations, Federal Register, and daily issuances of agency.

C.   THE CODE OF FEDERAL REGULATIONS

The Code of Federal Regulations (C.F.R.) is a compilation of the rules and regulations of the federal agencies.

What Does the C.F.R. Contain?	• Agency rules and regulations.
Relationship Between C.F.R. and Federal Register?	• C.F.R. is the codification of portions of the Federal Register.
Relationship Between C.F.R. and Statutes?	• C.F.R. contains the agency regulations that implement the legislation to which they relate. • Title number of C.F.R. is often the same as the related statute, but this is not always the case.
When Does the C.F.R. Issue?	• Once per year.
How is the C.F.R. Organized?	• 50 Titles, divided by subject matter. • Titles are divided into chapters, parts, and sections.
How to Use the C.F.R.?	• C.F.R. Index — by topic, agency, U.S.C. citation, Statutes at Large citation, Public Law number, and list of C.F.R. titles, chapters, sub-chapters, parts. • Index updated two times per year to reflect changes to regulations as of January 1 and July 1. • U.S.C.S. Index and Finding Aids to C.F.R. — by topic, U.S.C. citation, C.F.R. citation, statutes at large citation, list of C.F.R. titles, chapters, sub-chapters, and parts, agency, list of agency by C.F.R. title.
How to Locate Cases Relevant to Agency Rules and Regulations?	• Check case annotations to implementing statute in U.S.C.A. or U.S.C.S. • Consult looseleaf services relating to that area of law. • Update the regulation, using Shepard's Citators or similar service.

D. THE FEDERAL REGISTER

The Federal Register is a daily publication of regulations, rules, notices, and other agency and official issuances. Certain documents published in the Federal Register become published, or "codified" in the Code of Federal Regulations. See Part III.C.

What Does the Federal Register Contain?	• Agency and other executive branch pronouncements:
	  ○ The President:
	    ■ Executive orders.
	    ■ Presidential proclamations.
	    ■ Other presidential documents.
	  ○ Federal Agencies:
	    ■ Rules and regulations.
	    ■ General statements of policy.
	    ■ Notice of proposed rulemakings.
	    ■ Miscellaneous notices.
	    ■ Etc.
	• See C.F.R. Part 1.

When Does the Federal Register Issue?	• Daily.
How to Use the Federal Register?	• Consult daily list of parts of C.F.R. affected by C.F.R. title number and part number. • Monthly list of sections affected. • December index; or latest month's index plus daily issuances since the end of that month. • Subject indices — cumulative; updated annually.
Relationship Between Federal Register and C.F.R.?	• Federal Register can be viewed as the "pocket part" or daily supplement to the C.F.R. (including List of Sections Affected). • Rules and regulations ultimately get "codified" in the C.F.R.

E. PRESIDENTIAL DOCUMENTS

Executive Orders	• Directives to federal government employees. • Have force and effect of law. • May not legislate or override congressional action.
Presidential Proclamations	• "Softer" presidential statements. • Often involve "housekeeping" matters. • May commemorate person, place, or event.
Presidential Legislative Statements	• Presidential statements accompanying signing or vetoing of legislation.

Chapter 4

JUDICIAL SYSTEMS AND CASE LAW

This chapter covers the following:
- U.S. Judicial Systems (A.)
- Working with Case Law (B.)

A. U.S. JUDICIAL SYSTEMS

This part covers the following:
- Multiple Judicial Systems (1.)
- Federal Judicial System (2.)
- State Judicial Systems (3.)
- Exclusive and Concurrent/Overlapping Jurisdiction (4.)

1. Multiple Judicial Systems

Several Judicial Systems	• Federal judicial system. • State systems: ○ Each of the 50 states and territories has its own independent judicial system.
Federal Judicial System	• Product of U.S. Constitution and federal law. • See Chapter 1.A.4.b.
State Judicial Systems	• Products of respective state constitutions and state laws. • See Part A.3.

Parallel Judicial Systems	• Most cases go through one judicial system — federal or state — or the other.
	• Exceptions:
	  ○ *Certiorari* — U.S. Supreme Court may review decisions of state court of last resort that involve questions of federal law.
	  ○ *Habeas corpus* — federal district court may review claims of unconstitutional detention after review by state court of last resort.
	  ○ Certification — federal court may "certify" specific state law question to state court for resolution pursuant to state law.

2. Federal Judicial System

This section covers the following:

- General Attributes (a.)
- Subject Matter Jurisdiction of the Federal Courts (b.)
- Justiciability — The Case or Controversy Requirement in Federal Courts (c.)
- General Organization of the Federal Courts (d.)
- Map of the Geographic Boundaries of the U.S. Courts of Appeals and the U.S. District Courts (e.)
- The Supreme Court of the United States (f.)
- The United States Courts of Appeals (g.)
- The United States District Courts (h.)

a. General Attributes

Foundation	• Article III of the Constitution of the United States of America. • Federal statutory law, especially Title 28 of the United States Code.

Organization	• Constitutional basis:
	  ○ One Supreme Court.
	  ○ Congress given power to establish "inferior" federal courts.
	• Current organization:
	  ○ Hierarchical:
	    ■ Shape of a pyramid.
	    ■ See Part A.2.d.
	  ○ Geographic:
	    ■ District courts and courts of appeals covering different geographic regions.
	    ■ Supreme Court with nationwide jurisdiction.
	    ■ See Part A.2.d.

Selection of Federal Judges	• No stated qualifications in Constitution.
	• No special career track:
	  ○ Federal judges chosen from practice, academia, state judiciaries, etc.
	  ○ Federal judges typically have a good deal of legal experience before being nominated to the bench.
	• Process:
	  ○ Nomination by the President.
	  ○ Confirmation ("advice and consent") by Senate.

Judicial Independence	• No diminution in salary.
	• Tenure "during good Behaviour":
	   ○ Life tenure, absent conviction on impeachment.
	   ○ See Chapter 1.A.2.c.

Courts of General Jurisdiction	• Most federal courts are courts of general jurisdiction as opposed to specialized courts. • See Part A.2.d. regarding specialized courts.

Courts of Limited Jurisdiction	• Two limits on federal court jurisdiction:
	   ○ Subject matter jurisdiction — see Part A.2.b.
	   ○ Justiciability — the Case or Controversy requirement. See Part A.2.c.

b.   Subject Matter Jurisdiction of the Federal Courts

Limited Subject Matter Jurisdiction	• Consistent with federalism, federal courts have limited subject matter jurisdiction

Federal Question Jurisdiction	• Federal courts have jurisdiction to hear cases that "arise under" federal law:
	   ○ Constitutional.
	   ○ Statutory.

Diversity Jurisdiction	• Federal courts have jurisdiction to hear cases in which:
	   ○ Parties are citizens of different states; and
	   ○ The amount in controversy exceeds $75,000.

U.S. a Party	• Federal courts have jurisdiction to hear cases in which the U.S. is a party.
Other Cases	• Cases affecting ambassadors, other public ministers and consuls. • Cases of admiralty and maritime jurisdiction.
Supplemental Jurisdiction	• Federal courts have discretion to hear state law claims related to federal claims properly brought.
Removal Jurisdiction	• Defendant can "remove" case from state to federal court if it could originally have been brought in federal court: ○ Except if case is brought in defendant's home state court.

c.   Justiciability — The Case or Controversy Requirement in Federal Courts

Justiciability Defined	• Appropriateness of a dispute for judicial resolution. • U.S. courts do not issue advisory opinions.
Constitutional Foundation	• Article III section 2 requirement of "Cases" or "Controversies."

Impact of Lack of Justiciability	• Court will dismiss a case in which any of the justifiability requirements are not met.
Burden of Proof	• Party invoking federal jurisdiction bears the burden of establishing that the claim is justiciable.

Requirements of Justiciability	• Requirements of Justiciability:
	  ○ Standing.
	  ○ Ripeness.
	  ○ Non-Mootness.
	  ○ No Political Questions.
	• See discussion of each requirement immediately below.

Standing	• Issue = is plaintiff proper party to bring claim?
	• General rule: parties must have an actual, cognizable interest in the outcome of the litigation.
	• Requirements:
	  ○ Plaintiff must have suffered an "injury in fact," which is "concrete and particularized" and which is "actual or imminent" rather than "conjectural or hypothetical";
	  ○ There must be a "causal connection between the injury and the conduct complained of"; and
	  ○ It must be likely that the injury will be "redressed by a favorable decision" of the court.

Ripeness	• Issue = has the claim matured to the point where it is appropriate for judicial resolution?
	• General rule:
	  ○ The dispute must present a current controversy that has immediate rather than anticipated or hypothetical effects on the parties.
	  ○ In cases involving administrative agencies:
	    ■ Agency decision must be final.
	    ■ Party seeking review must have exhausted all possible avenues of relief before the administrative body.
	• Considerations/factors:
	  ○ Whether the factual record is sufficient to permit adjudication of the merits of the claim;
	  ○ Whether delaying adjudication will cause hardship to the plaintiff;
	  ○ Likelihood that hardship to plaintiff will come to pass if adjudication is delayed; and
	  ○ Public interest in adjudication at the present time.
	• Among other things, the ripeness doctrine generally precludes a court from giving pre-enforcement review of a statute or regulation.

Non-Mootness	• Issue = whether a dispute has become moot or obsolete and thus no longer merits judicial resolution because it has ceased to involve a current, live controversy. • Inverse of ripeness doctrine. • Exceptions: ○ Voluntary cessation of challenged activity, which could be resumed at any time. ○ Alleged injury that is "capable of repetition yet evading review."
Political Question Doctrine	• Issue: ○ Whether a case raises a political question that has been left to the resolution of the political branches and thus is inappropriate for judicial intervention. ○ Implicates separation of powers concerns. • Limited doctrine — does not mean that cases of a political nature or involving political issues are exempt from judicial review. • Examples of Political Questions that will not be reviewed by the courts: ○ Constitutional guarantee of a "republican form of government." ○ President's exercise of power over military and foreign affairs. ○ Way in which Congress carries out impeachment proceedings.

d. General Organization of the Federal Courts

How Organized	• Hierarchy; and • Geography.
Hierarchical Structure	• Shape of a pyramid: ○ U.S. District Courts at base (see Part A.2.h.). ○ U.S. Courts of Appeals in center (see Part A.2.g.). ○ Supreme Court of the United States at apex (see Part A.2.f.).
Geographical Structure	• 94 judicial districts. • 12 regionally-based intermediate appellate courts. • Single Supreme Court.
Concept of a Circuit	• Circuit = geographic region containing one federal regional court of appeals and some number of district courts. • Appeals from district court must be taken to court of appeals in same circuit. • Important for application of rules of *stare decisis* (see Part B.3.).

Specialized Courts	• Specialized courts at the trial level:
	○ Bankruptcy courts:
	■ Located within federal judicial districts.
	■ Hear matters relating to bankruptcy law.
	■ Non-Article III courts.
	○ Court of International Trade:
	■ Located in New York City.
	■ Broad nationwide jurisdiction to hear civil actions pertaining to international trade issues.
	○ Tax Court:
	■ Hears taxpayer appeals from tax deficiencies determined by Commissioner of Internal Revenue, among other tax matters.
	■ Non-Article III court.
	○ Court of Federal Claims:
	■ Located in Washington, D.C.
	■ Nationwide jurisdiction over various money claims against the United States in excess of $10,000, for example, cases involving the following:
	✓ Government contracts.
	✓ Constitutional claims.
	✓ Tax refunds.
	✓ Indian claims.
	✓ Civilian and military pay claims.
	✓ Patent and copyright matters.
	✓ Vaccine injury claims.
	• Specialized courts at the appellate level:
	○ Federal Circuit:
	■ Located in Washington, D.C.
	■ Nationwide jurisdiction over a number of types of cases, including those involving international trade, government contracts, patents, certain money claims against the U.S. government, federal personnel, and veterans' benefits.
	■ Appeals come from:
	✓ Federal district courts.
	✓ United States Court of Federal Claims.
	✓ United States Court of International Trade.
	✓ United States Court of Appeals for Veterans Claims.
	✓ Certain administrative agencies.
	○ U.S. Court of Appeals for Veteran Claims:
	■ Exclusive jurisdiction over decisions of the Board of Veterans' Appeals.

	■ Located in Washington, D.C. but must sit anywhere in the U.S. ■ Non-Article III court.

e. **Map of the Geographic Boundaries of the U.S. Courts of Appeals and the U.S. District Courts**

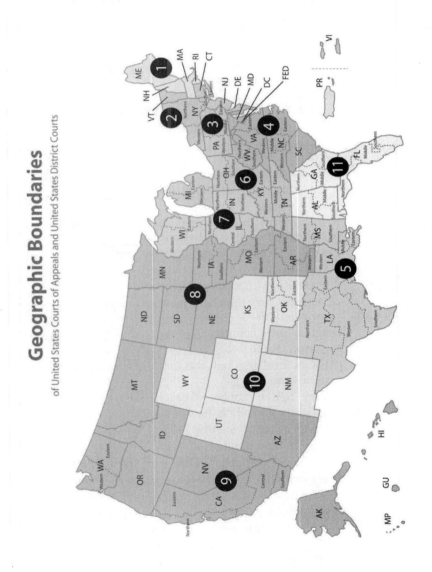

Source: http://www.uscourts.gov/uscourts/images/CircuitMap.pdf

f.   The Supreme Court of the United States

Formal Court Name	• Supreme Court of the United States. • Also referred to as the "Court" if reference is clear from the context.
Type of Court	• Court of last resort on questions of federal law. • Not ordinary court of error correction — more concerned with national uniformity on important questions of federal law.

Basic Court Structure	• Single Supreme Court.
	 • Nine Justices:
	    ○ 1 Chief Justice.
	    ○ 8 Associate Justices.
	 • Sits *en banc*:
	    ○ All Justices hear and decide each case;
	    ○ Unless recused/disqualified for real or perceived conflict of interest.

Term	• Session:
	    ○ Begins first Monday in October.
	    ○ Ends late June/first days of July.

Where do Cases Come from?	• Federal courts of appeals. • State courts of last resort if state court decision based on question(s) of federal law.

Jurisdiction	• Forms of Supreme Court Jurisdiction:
	    ○ Original jurisdiction.
	    ○ Mandatory appellate jurisdiction.
	    ○ Discretionary appellate jurisdiction (*certiorari* jurisdiction).
	 • Original Jurisdiction:
	    ○ State v. State.
	    ○ Cases involving ambassadors, consuls, other public ministers.
	    ○ Very limited number of cases.
	 • Mandatory Appellate Jurisdiction:
	    ○ Cases as prescribed by federal legislation.
	    ○ Very limited number of cases.
	 • Discretionary Appellate/*Certiorari* Jurisdiction
	    ○ Majority of cases that come to the Supreme Court.
	    ○ Vehicle = petition for a writ of *certiorari*:
	      ▪ Approximately 10,000 petitions filed per year.
	      ▪ 75–80 petitions typically granted.
	    ○ "Rule of Four" — petition for writ of *certiorari* granted if four Justices vote in favor.
	    ○ No reason given for denial of writ of *certiorari*.

	○ Reasons for granting writ of *certiorari* include split among lower courts on important question of federal law.
Reporters	• United States Reports — U.S. [official]. • Supreme Court Reporter — S. Ct. [West]. • Lawyers' Edition — L. Ed. [Lawyers' Cooperative]. • United States Law Week/Supreme Court Bulletin — newest Court decisions.
Digests	• United States Supreme Court Digest [West]. • Federal Practice Digest [currently in 5th series] [West]. • Modern Federal Practice Digest [older cases] [West]. • Federal Digest [older cases] [West].
Applicable Statutes And Rules	• Rules of the United States Supreme Court. • Title 28 of the United States Code.

g.   The United States Courts of Appeals

Formal Court Name	• United States Court of Appeals. • United States Court of Appeals for the [__] Circuit. • Also referred to as the Circuit Court.

Type of Court	• Intermediate court of appeals:
	   ○ Right of appeal by party aggrieved by district court decision.
	   ○ Initial court review of appeals from some agency actions.

Basic Court Structure	• 12 geographically-based courts of appeals, one for each circuit:
	   ○ 1st through 11th Circuits.
	   ○ Court of Appeals for the District of Columbia Circuit.
	 • 6–28 court of appeals judges per circuit.

Access to Court	• Direct appeal from final determinations of district courts. • Direct review of final action of some federal agencies when provided for in enabling legislation.

Decision-Making	• 3-judge panel.
	 • *En banc* review:
	   ○ Discretionary review of 3-judge panel decision.
	   ○ In most circuits, all judges on that court of appeals will review decision.
	   ○ Issues of law only.

Reporter	• Federal Reporter — F./F.2d./F.3d [West]

Digests	• Federal Practice Digest [currently in 5th series] [West]. • Modern Federal Practice Digest [older cases] [West]. • Federal Digest [older cases] [West].
Applicable Statutes and Rules	• Title 28 of the United States Code. • Federal Rules of Appellate Procedure — applicable to all circuits. • Local court rules adopted by and applicable within each circuit. See Fed. R. App. Proc. 47.

h.   The United States District Courts

Basic Court Structure	• 94 District Courts:
	    ○ 1–4 per state, as established by Congress.
	 • How named:
	    ○ 1 in state = United States District Court for the District of [State].
	    ○ More than 1 in a state = United States District Court for the [Eastern, Western, Northern, Southern, Central] District of [State].

Number of Judges	• 1–28 per district, as established by Congress. • Each case heard by a single judge.
Principal Function	• Trial-level courts. • Principal function is fact-finding. • Also decides dispositive legal issues.

Jury	• Right to a trial by jury:
	    ○ Most criminal cases.
	    ○ Civil cases in which money damages sought.
	 • Jury decides questions of fact.
	 • Right to jury trial may be waived by the parties.
	    ○ Judge decides questions of fact.
	    ○ "Bench" trial.

Reporters	• Federal Supplement — F. Supp./F. Supp. 2d/F. Supp. 3d [West]. • Federal Rules Decisions (selected district court cases on procedural issues) — FRD [West].
Digests	• Federal Practice Digest [currently in 5th series] [West]. • Modern Federal Practice Digest [older cases] [West]. • Federal Digest [older cases] [West].
Applicable Statutes and Rules	• Title 28 of the United States Code. • Federal Rules of Civil Procedure. • Federal Rules of Evidence. • Local court rules adopted by and applicable within each district. See Fed. R. Civ. Proc. 83.

Access to Court	• Initial level of court review. • *Habeas corpus* review from state court covering same geographic area.

3. State Judicial Systems

Variations Among States	• State judicial systems are the product of state law: ○ Variations, often significant, exist from system to system with regard to court structure, rules of procedure and evidence, how judges are selected, rules of *stare decisis*, etc.
Typical Organization of State Judicial Systems	• Most state court systems, like the federal system, have a three-tiered structure: ○ Trial-level courts. ○ Intermediate appellate courts. ○ Court of last resort (often but not always called the Supreme Court).
Judicial Selection and Terms	• Procedures for selecting state judges: ○ Selected (often by governor or mayors at local level). ○ Elections. • Judges serve for defined terms, but typically not for life.
Specialized Courts	• State judicial systems commonly have more specialized courts than in the federal system. • Examples: ○ Commercial courts. ○ Criminal courts. ○ Family courts. ○ Probate courts. ○ Juvenile courts. ○ Small claim courts.
State Reporters	• State: ○ Official state and/or West case reporter. ○ Typically report cases from intermediate appellate and high court. • Regional: ○ West regional reporters. ○ Combine cases from several states into one reporter. ○ Organization of states does not mirror organization of federal circuits. • Details of state and regional reporter systems can be found in *Bluebook* or *ALWD Citation Manual*.

State Digests	• State:
	   ○ Official state and/or West case digest
	• Regional:
	   ○ Some state cases are digested in West regional reporters

State Court Rules of Practice and Procedure	• Each state also has its own rules of practice and procedure applicable to each court. • Most states will have annotated versions of their rules of practice and procedure, or practice guides explaining the application of such rules.

4. Exclusive and Concurrent/Overlapping Jurisdiction

Exclusive Federal Court Jurisdiction	• Congress by statute may prescribe that federal courts shall have exclusive jurisdiction. • Case can be brought only in federal court.

Overlapping/ Concurrent Jurisdiction	• Exists when:
	   ○ Basis for federal court jurisdiction (see Section A.2.b.); *and*
	   ○ No statutory requirement of exclusive federal court jurisdiction.
	• Case can be brought in federal or state court.
	   ○ Defendant can exercise removal jurisdiction if case filed in state court that is not defendant's home. See Section A.2.b.

Exclusive State Court Jurisdiction	• No basis for federal court jurisdiction. • Case must be brought in state court.

B. WORKING WITH CASE LAW

This part addresses the following:

- Elements of a Judicial Opinion (1.)
- Syllabus and Headnotes (2.)
- *Stare Decisis* (3.)
- Identifying and Working with *Dictum* (4.)
- Analogizing and Distinguishing Precedent (5.)
- Dealing with Contrary Authority (6.)

1. Elements of a Judicial Opinion

The following are commonly found in published judicial opinions:

Case Citation	• Address for the case; directs parties to the place or places where the opinion is published. • See Chapter 6.E.
Court	• Court issuing the decision.
Parties	• Names. • Litigation position (*e.g.*, plaintiff, defendant, appellant, appellee, petitioner, respondent).
Docket Number	• Number that the court uses to identify and file the case. • Not relevant for readers of judicial opinions.
Date	• Date of decision. • Only year is relevant. • May also indicate date of oral argument, if held.
Attorneys	• Names, firms, and addresses of attorneys of record.

Author of Opinion	• Judge who wrote decision.
	• Cases on appeal:
	  ○ Name of the primary author of the opinion of the court and, often, other members of the panel.
	  ○ May be issued *per curiam* or "by the court."

Syllabus and Headnotes	• Depending on the publisher of the reporter, the case may contain:
	  ○ Syllabus, which is a summary of the decision; and
	  ○ Headnotes, or brief summaries of specific points made in the opinion.
	• These are not part of the court's decision and may not be relied upon or quoted or cited.
	• See Part B.2.

Opinion of the Court	• Opinion of the trial court judge or a majority of the members of an appellate panel.
	• Will generally contain the following elements:
	  ○ Procedural history.
	  ○ Issue(s).
	  ○ Facts.
	  ○ Law:
	    ■ Statement of the rule(s) of law to be applied.
	  ○ Discussion:
	    ■ Analysis of the facts as applied to the applicable law.
	    ■ Discussion of both positions.
	  ○ Holding = answer to legal issue(s) presented.
	  ○ Rationale = reasoning to justify the holding.
	  ○ Conclusion.

Dissenting Opinion (sometimes)	• Opinion of one or more judges on appeal who disagree(s) with the outcome reached by the majority.
Concurring Opinion (sometimes)	• Opinion of one of more judges on appeal who agree(s) with the outcome reached by the majority but for a different or additional reason.

2. Syllabus and Headnotes

Syllabus	• Summary of decision that precedes opinion. • Found in many reporters.

Headnotes	• Brief summaries of particular points of law discussed in the opinion.
	• Found after the syllabus and before the opinion of the court.
	• Typically a case will have several, and in some cases many, headnotes.
	• Not written by the court but by legal publishers.
	• No legal standing — may not be relied upon or cited.
	• Value:
	  ○ Summarize relevant portion of opinion.
	  ○ Useful in finding portions of opinion in which particular issues are addressed.
	  ○ Allow reader to access other cases dealing with the same legal topic/issue.
	  ○ West headnotes link directly to West digest system.

3. *Stare Decisis*

This section discusses the following:

- *Stare Decisis* in General (a.)
- Some Rules Regarding the Application of *Stare Decisis* Principles (b.)
- Summary of Precedential Effect of Federal Court Decisions on Matters of Federal Law (c.)

a. *Stare Decisis* in General

Defined	• "Let it stand." • Tendency of U.S. courts to follow principles of law announced in earlier judicial decisions.

Rationale	• Fairness/check on arbitrary behavior — similar cases should be decided in a similar way. • Judicial economy — allows courts to rely on principles of law settled in earlier cases. • Predictability — allows parties to better anticipate their chances of success and to evaluate settlement strategies more effectively.

Precedent May Be Binding or Persuasive	• Binding = mandatory = controlling = must be followed by court.
	• Persuasive:
	  ○ Should be consulted by court in absence of binding authority.
	  ○ Court may but need not follow it.

Factors in *Stare Decisis* Analysis	• Factors:
	  ○ Facts.
	  ○ Legal issue(s).
	  ○ Relationship between court(s) issuing precedent and current court.
	  ○ Whether legal principle was related to the earlier court's holding or is *dictum*.
	• Each factor is discussed immediately below.

Facts	• *Stare decisis* applies to cases that are factually similar.
	• Parties use facts to analogize and distinguish facts of prior cases.
	• Analogize:
	  ○ Party that wants precedent to be applied argues to the court that the facts of the earlier case(s) are analogous/materially similar to the facts presented.
	• Distinguish:
	  ○ Party that does not want precedent to be applied argues to the court that the facts of the earlier case(s) are readily distinguishable/different from the facts presented in legally significant ways.
	• See Part B.5.

Legal Issue(s)	• Legal issue(s) must be the same or similar for *stare decisis* to apply.

Relationship Between Courts	• Application of *stare decisis* depends on relationship between issuing court(s) and current court.
	• Must consider:
	  ○ Hierarchy; and
	  ○ Jurisdiction.
	• Hierarchy:
	  ○ In general, higher-level courts bind lower level courts.
	  ○ Courts at the same level may be binding.

	• Jurisdiction:
	  ○ Place from which court decision arose.
	  ○ Cases are binding only within the same jurisdiction.
	  ○ Relevant inquiry:
	    ■ Federal court — which district or circuit?
	    ■ State court — which state?
	• See Part B.3.c.

Holding or *Dictum*	• Holding = court's answer(s) to the legal issue(s) presented. • *Dictum* = statements that a court may make that go beyond the facts or legal issues under consideration. • See Part B.4.

b. Some Rules Regarding the Application of *Stare Decisis* Principles

i. Rules Regarding Federal Law

Decisions of U.S. Supreme Court	• Binding on all inferior federal courts.
	• Binding on all state courts.
	• How overruled:
	  ○ Supreme Court generally follows its own precedent but may overrule its earlier decisions, expressly or by implication.
	  ○ Cases involving statutory law may be prospectively overruled by acts of Congress.

Decisions of U.S. Courts of Appeals	• Binding within the circuit:
	  ○ District courts in that circuit.
	  ○ That court of appeals itself.
	• Persuasive authority for all other courts, including other federal courts of appeals and district courts located in other circuits.
	• How overruled:
	  ○ Court of appeals itself, sitting *en banc*. See Part A.2.g.
	  ○ Supreme Court.
	  ○ Cases involving statutory law may be prospectively overruled by acts of Congress.

Decisions of U.S. District Courts	• Binding only on the parties, subject to any decisions on appeal. • Persuasive authority for all other courts.

ii.   Rules Regarding State Law

In General	• A state court of last resort is the ultimate judicial arbiter of the interpretation and application of the laws of that state.
Decisions of State Court of Last Resort	• Federal and state courts interpreting law of State X must "stand in the shoes" of the highest court of the state and apply that state's law as they believe that court would apply it. • See discussion of certification in Part A.1.
Decisions of Lower State Courts	• Binding within the state as directed by state rules on precedent. • Persuasive authority for all other courts.
Decisions of the U.S. Supreme Court	• Binding on inferior federal courts, subject to any subsequent clarification by state court of last resort. • Persuasive authority for all other courts.
Decisions of U.S. Court of Appeals	• Binding within the circuit, subject to any subsequent clarification by state court of last resort. • Persuasive authority for all other courts.
Decisions of the U.S. District Court	• Binding only on the parties, subject to any decisions on appeal. • Persuasive authority for all other courts.

c.   Summary of Precedential Effect of Federal Court Decisions on Matters of Federal Law[*]

Precedent Established By:	In Subsequent Opinion By:	Precedential Effect:
U.S. Supreme Court	U.S. Supreme Court	Tendency to follow
U.S. Supreme Court	Any U.S. Court of Appeals	Binding
U.S. Supreme Court	Any U.S. District Court	Binding
U.S. Supreme Court	Any state court	Binding
U.S. Court of Appeals for the [X] Circuit	U.S. Supreme Court	Not binding — persuasive
U.S. Court of Appeals for the [X] Circuit	U.S. Court of Appeals for the [X] Circuit	Binding, unless overruled or reversed by Court of Appeals for the [X] Circuit sitting *en banc*.
U.S. Court of Appeals for the [X] Circuit	U.S. Court of Appeals for the [Y] Circuit	Not binding — persuasive
U.S. Court of Appeals for the [X] Circuit	U.S. District Courts in [X] Circuit	Binding

---

[*] Assumes no intervening Supreme Court precedent or relevant congressional action.

Precedent Established By:	In Subsequent Opinion By:	Precedential Effect:
U.S. Court of Appeals for the [X] Circuit	U.S. District Courts in [Y] Circuit	Not binding — persuasive
U.S. Court of Appeals for the [X] Circuit	Any state court	Not binding — persuasive
U.S. District Court for the District of A	U.S. Supreme Court	Not binding — persuasive
U.S. District Court for the District of A	Any U.S. Court of Appeals	Not binding — persuasive
U.S. District Court for the District of A	Any U.S. District Court	Not binding — persuasive
U.S. District Court for the District of A	Any state court	Not binding — persuasive

4.   Identifying and Working with *Dictum*

Dictum Defined	• Any part of a court's decision that deals with facts and/or issues not properly presented to the court. • "[s]tray observations." *Office of Consumers' Counsel, State of Ohio v. FERC*, 826 F.2d 1136, 1139 (D.C. Cir. 1987). • *Dicta* = plural of *dictum*.
Not Desirable	• Inconsistent with general rule that courts should deal only with concrete facts and issues properly presented for review.
Hard to Identify	• May be difficult to identify. • Parties may argue as to whether certain statements constitute *dictum* or part of the court's holding/rationale.
How Used	• Parties will argue as to extent to which *dictum* may have *stare decisis* impact. • Technically, never binding but subsequent courts may find certain *dictum* highly persuasive, especially if court gave careful consideration to issue that is the subject of the *dictum*.

5.   Analogizing and Distinguishing Precedent

Precedent Defined	• Earlier-decided cases. • Generally refers to cases involving the same legal issues and similar facts.

Analogizing versus Distinguishing	• Analogizing to precedent:
	  ○ Argue in favor of applying principle(s) announced in precedent.
	  ○ Show that material facts in precedent are essentially the same as in the present case and that court should reach the same result.
	• Distinguishing precedent:
	  ○ Argue against applying principle(s) announced in precedent.
	  ○ Show that material facts in precedent are distinguishable in important ways such that court should reach a different result.

Use by Parties	• Analogizing to precedent:
	  ○ Party that wants court to apply rule of law announced in precedent.
	• Distinguishing precedent:
	  ○ Party that wants court to reject rule of law announced in precedent and adopt a different rule.

How to Analogize to Precedent	• Material facts similar enough to warrant same result. • Depict holding as broad. • Similar policy reasons warrant same result.
How to Distinguish Precedent	• Material facts different in legally significant ways. • Depict holding as narrow. • Sound policy supports different result.

6. Dealing with Contrary Authority

Defined	• Legal authority that undermines one's own litigation position.
Ethical Obligation to Reveal	• Attorneys have an ethical obligation to reveal contrary authority to the court.

How to Negate Impact of Contrary Authority	• Facts — the material facts are distinguishable and therefore not applicable to the case at hand.
	• Issues — the legal issues differ.
	• Judicial authority — the contrary authority is not binding on the court before which your case appears.
	• Undermined by subsequent case law — the earlier precedent, while not directly overruled, has been effectively repudiated by the court that issued it or other courts.
	• Seek change — the precedent cited should be changed because:
	  ○ The weight of authority in other jurisdictions supports a contrary result.
	  ○ Policy considerations now support a change in the law.

How to Acknowledge in Interoffice Memorandum	• Discuss directly, consistent with the objective purpose of the memorandum. • Discuss the extent to which the impact of the contrary authority is minimized by any of the factors above. • Indicate the likely impact of the negative precedent on the outcome. • See Chapter 6.B.
How to Acknowledge in Court Documents	• Strategically preferable to reveal contrary authority before your opponent does. • Present the authority in a way that minimizes its negative impact to the extent possible. • Juxtapose the potentially contrary authority with an argument as to why it should not be the basis for an unfortunate ruling in your case. • See Chapter 6.C. and D.

Chapter 5

CIVIL LITIGATION AND APPEALS

This chapter covers the following:

- Party Designations and Their Roles in the Litigation and Appellate Processes (A.)
- Civil Litigation (B.)
- Appellate Litigation (C.)
- Court Issuances and Dispositions (D.)

This chapter uses as its source the rules of the federal courts. Civil litigation and appellate practice in many states draw inspiration from the federal rules, but significant differences may exist. It is of course vital to consult state laws and rules of practice and procedure when working in a particular state. In the federal courts, local court rules and orders should also be consulted.

A. PARTY DESIGNATIONS AND THEIR ROLES IN THE LITIGATION AND APPELLATE PROCESSES

The charts that follow show the designations of the parties and define their roles at each court level. Some designations may vary according to local practice.

1. Party Designations at U.S. District Court

Plaintiff	• Party bringing action for relief. • May be abbreviated as "P" or "Π."
Defendant	• Party against whom action is brought. • May be abbreviated as "D" or "Δ."
Counter-Claimant	• Defendant in posture of bringing counterclaim against plaintiff.
Cross-Claimant	• Defendant in posture of bringing claim against another defendant.
Third-Party Plaintiff	• Defendant that brings in a nonparty as allegedly being responsible for some or all of the claims against the third-party plaintiff.
Third-Party Defendant	• Party in posture of defending against claim by third-party plaintiff.

| Intervenor | • Interested party participating in litigation upon permission of the court or as stipulated by law.
• Intervention as of right:
  ○ Unconditional right to intervene by statute.
  ○ Person who claims interest relating to property or transaction that is the subject of the action and whose rights may be impaired by the action.
• Permissible intervention:
  ○ Has claim or defense that shares with the main action a common question of law or fact.
  ○ Government officer or agency.
  ○ Other cases at the discretion of the judge. |

2. Party Designations at U.S. Court of Appeals

Appellant	• Party bringing appeal. • Was at least in part unsuccessful in the proceedings below.
Appellee	• Party against which appeal is sought. • Party that was at least in part successful in the proceedings below. • Party defending trial court ruling.
Petitioner	• Party challenging agency action. • Was at least in part unsuccessful in the proceedings below.
Respondent	• Agency whose action is being challenged. • Defends agency action under review.
Intervenor	• Intervenors in the district court are typically granted intervenor status in the court of appeals. • In the case of review of agency action, intervenors will be parties to the agency process below.

Amicus Curiae	• "Friend of the court."
	• Who may file:
	  ○ U.S. or agency or officer thereof.
	  ○ Anyone else, by leave of court or consent of all parties. Should demonstrate:
	    ■ Moving part's interest; and
	    ■ Why *amicus* brief is desirable and why the matters asserted are relevant to the disposition of the case.

3.   Party Designations at Supreme Court of the United Sates

Petitioner	• Party seeking Supreme Court review and, if granted, urging rejection of the court's decision below. • Party that was at least in part unsuccessful in the proceedings below.
Respondent	• Party opposing Supreme Court review. • If Supreme Court review granted, party defending resolution of the decision below. • Party that was at least in part successful in the proceedings below.
Intervenor	• Motion for leave to intervene permitted. • Supreme Court rules do not provide standard for granting of motion.

Amicus curiae	• "Friend of the Court."
	• Who may file:
	  ○ Person/group/entity who has written consent of all parties.
	  ○ Person/group/entity who receives leave from the Court to file an *amicus* brief.
	  ○ The United States by the Solicitor General or someone authorized to file on behalf of any U.S. agency.
	  ○ A state, when submitted by the state's attorney general.
	  ○ A locality, when submitted by its authorized law officer.
	• Brief should "bring[] to the attention of the Court relevant matter not already brought to its attention by the parties."

U.S. Solicitor General	• Office of Solicitor General supervises and conducts litigation in the U.S. Supreme Court. • May participate in *certiorari* practice, briefing, and argument.

B.   CIVIL LITIGATION

This part addresses the following points:

- Preliminary Points Relating to the Federal Civil Litigation Process (1.)
- Civil Litigation Process (2.)

1. Preliminary Points Relating to the Federal Civil Litigation Process

Scope/Definition	• Includes all disputes submitted to a court.
	• May seek monetary damages, specific performance, or forbearance from specific activity.
	• Distinguished from:
	  ○ Administrative proceedings before an agency, board, or other body.
	  ○ Criminal litigation, in which the government seeks sanctions against a person for violation of a criminal law.
	  ○ Appellate litigation, which is the process by which a higher court reviews decisions made by a lower court. See Part C.

Federal Rules of Civil Procedure [Fed. R. Civ. Proc. or FRCP]	• Primary source of procedural rules for litigation in the federal district courts. • Supplemented by local court rules and individual judge's orders.
Federal Rules of Evidence	• Primary source of evidentiary rules for litigation in the federal district court.

Jurisdiction and Venue	• Issues of jurisdiction and venue critical to the filing of a complaint.
	• Jurisdiction:
	  ○ Subject-matter jurisdiction — the authority of the court to hear the type of case presented.
	  ○ Personal jurisdiction — whether the court has the authority to compel the presence in that court of an out-of-state defendant.
	• Venue:
	  ○ The place where a case will be heard.
	  ○ Geographic distribution of cases within a particular jurisdiction, *e.g.*, in a particular district.
	• Federal court jurisdiction and venue provisions are found in Title 28 of the United States Code.

Certificate of Service	• As a general matter, a party submitting any document in court must submit a Certificate of Service reflecting that a copy of the document has been served on the opposing party/parties.
Issues of Timing	• Consult statutes, court rules, and judicial orders relating to time limits and deadlines. • Some deadlines are jurisdictional and cannot be waived by the parties or the court.

2. Civil Litigation Process

The following chart describes the typical civil litigation process in federal court (*i.e.*, in a United States District Court).

Complaint [Fed. R. Civ. Proc. 7, 8]	• Filed by plaintiff to commence lawsuit.
	• Consists of individually numbered allegations.
	• Contains following elements:
	  ○ Identifies parties.
	  ○ Establishes grounds for jurisdiction and venue.
	  ○ Identifies cause(s) of action.
	  ○ Requests specific relief.
	  ○ Preserves right to trial by jury.
	• Modern "notice pleading" does not require that counsel set forth elaborate facts or grounds for relief.
	• Failure to investigate to ensure that the bringing of a lawsuit is not frivolous may lead to sanctions upon the attorney pursuant to Rule 11 of the Federal Rules of Civil Procedure.

Summons [Fed. R. Civ. Proc. 4]	• Order by the court clerk made upon the filing of the complaint. • Requires response by defendant by indicated deadline.
Service [Fed. R. Civ. Proc. 4]	• Plaintiff must arrange for complaint and summons to be delivered to other party or parties to lawsuit. • Methods of acceptable service stipulated by rule.

Answer [Fed. R. Civ. Proc. 7, 8]	• Filed by defendant in response to complaint.
	• Responds in order to each allegation in complaint in matching numbered paragraphs.
	• Must include all affirmative defenses.
	  ○ Affirmative defense = set of facts other than those alleged in complaint which, if proven, would defeat or mitigate any otherwise unlawful conduct.
	  ○ Examples:
	    ■ Statute of limitations.
	    ■ Statute of frauds.
	    ■ Waiver.
	    ■ Lack of personal jurisdiction.
	• May include counterclaim and/or cross-claim. See below.
	• Defendant may file a motion to dismiss in lieu of a traditional answer. See below.

Reply [Fed. R. Civ. Proc. 7, 8]	• Reply by plaintiff is required if the answer contains a counterclaim. • Plaintiff may also make reply with permission of the court.

Counterclaim [Fed. R. Civ. Proc. 13(a–e)]	• Claim by any party against an opposing party (*e.g.*, defendant versus plaintiff).
	• Types of counterclaims:
	 ○ "Compulsory":
	  ■ Arises out of same transaction or occurrence.
	  ■ Waived if not raised now.
	 ○ "Permissive":
	  ■ Does not arise out of same transaction or occurrence.
	  ■ May be made now or at some later time.

Cross-Claim [Fed. R. Civ. Proc. 13(g)]	• Claim by one party against a co-party (*e.g.*, one defendant against another defendant) arising out of the same transaction or subject matter of the original action or any counterclaim thereto.
Joinder [Fed. R. Civ. Proc. 20]	• Persons/entities may be added to a proceeding as plaintiffs or defendants.
Intervention [Fed. R. Civ. Proc. 24]	• Process by which interested person not named in lawsuit seeks court order allowing its participation. • Normally, intervenors may not introduce into the proceedings issues not raised by the principal parties. • Types of intervention: ○ Intervention of Right — when provided by statute. ○ Permissive Intervention — when a party has a "claim or defense that shares with the main action a common question of law or fact." Fed. R. Civ. Proc. 24(b).
Motion to Dismiss [Fed. R. Civ. Proc. 12(b)]	• Grounds upon which dismissal may be sought: ○ Lack of subject-matter jurisdiction (see below). ○ Lack of personal jurisdiction. ○ Improper venue. ○ Insufficiency of process. ○ Insufficiency of service of process. ○ Failure to state a claim upon which relief can be granted (see below). ○ Failure to join a necessary party. • Motion to Dismiss for Lack of Subject Matter Jurisdiction: ○ May be raised at any time. ○ Implicates the authority of the court and cannot be waived. ○ May be raised *sua sponte* by the court (*i.e.*, on the court's own motion). • Motion to Dismiss for Failure to State a Claim upon Which Relief Can Be Granted: ○ Even if all facts pleaded are true, there is no cause of action.

	○ May be filed by any party against whom a claim has been filed (defendant, counterclaimant, cross-claimant). ○ If granted, case is over as to that claim — moving party wins on the merits.

Discovery [Fed. R. Civ. Proc. 26–37]	• In general:
	 ○ Fact-gathering process that occurs pre-trial.
	 ○ Engaged in by all parties.
	 ○ Automatic disclosure required as to certain basic information and documents pertaining to the case; no request need be made.
	 ○ May be extremely expensive and time-consuming.
	 ○ Party-driven — court largely absent from discovery process.
	 • Extensive scope:
	 ○ "Parties may obtain discovery regarding any nonprivileged matter that is relevant to any party's claim or defense . . . . Relevant information need not be admissible at the trial if the discovery appears reasonably calculated to lead to the discovery of admissible evidence." Fed. R. Civ. Proc. 26(b)(1).
	 • Principal forms of discovery:
	 ○ Written Interrogatories — Fed. R. Civ. Proc. 33:
	   ■ Written questions seeking written responses.
	 ○ Requests for the Production of Documents and Things — Fed. R. Civ. Proc. 34:
	   ■ Written request to produce documents and other items related to the litigation.
	   ■ Response is usually an invitation to review documents to be made available by responding party.
	 ○ Physical and Mental Examinations — Fed. R. Civ. Proc. 35:
	   ■ When relevant to case.
	 ○ Requests to Admit — Fed. R. Civ. Proc. 36:
	   ■ Written allegations which recipient is to admit or deny, in writing.
	   ■ Failure to do so by prescribed time will result in allegations being "deemed admitted."
	   ■ Cost of proving allegations not admitted but which should have been falls on recipient.
	 ○ Oral Depositions — Fed. R. Civ. Proc. 30:
	   ■ Verbal answers given under oath to oral questions.
	 • When discovery occurs:
	 ○ Right to discovery attaches upon filing of lawsuit.

- o Discovery often lasts for years and delays trial date or other merits disposition accordingly.
- o Courts impose deadlines by which discovery shall have taken place.
- Advantages and disadvantages of extensive pre-trial discovery:
  - o Advantages:
    - Allows better trial preparation.
    - Allows parties to better evaluate their settlement posture.
  - o Disadvantages:
    - May be exploited; can become a "fishing expedition."
- Discovery motions:
  - o Motions to Compel Discovery — request that court order recipient of discovery request to provide answers or more complete/responsive answers. Fed. R. Civ. Proc. 37(a).
  - o Motion for Protective Order:
    - Request that court not require response by recipient of discovery request.
    - Grounds may include that the requests are overbroad or irrelevant, or that disclosure would violate the attorney-client privilege or would require disclosure of attorney work product.
    - May also request that court impose limits on who can view certain discovery responses or order that responding party may redact sensitive information from discovery disclosure.
    - Fed. R. Civ. Proc. 26(c).
  - o Courts generally look with extreme displeasure on the filing of motions for protective orders and motions to compel discovery.
    - The parties are expected to make every effort to resolve discovery conflicts on their own before resorting to court intervention.
- Privileges from discovery:
  - o Attorney work product:
    - Protects from discovery material prepared by or for a party or a party's representative in anticipation of litigation.
    - Limited exception for some attorney work product upon showing of need.
    - No exception for mental impression work product — work product that contains the attorney's mental impressions, conclusions, opinions, or legal theories.

	○ Attorney-client communications: ■ Confidential communications made between an attorney and client/prospective client in the course of seeking legal counsel is privileged and immune from discovery.
Motion for Summary Judgment [Fed. R. Civ. Proc. 56]	• Basis for motion: ○ The facts are not sufficiently in dispute and therefore there is no reason for the court to waste the resources in impaneling jury. ○ No reasonable jury could find for non-moving party. • Who may file: ○ May be filed by either party. ○ Cross-motions sometimes filed by both parties. • Full or partial: ○ Full — relating to entire case. ○ Partial — relating to some portion(s) of the case. • If moving party wins complete motion for summary judgment, the case is over in favor of the moving party. • If summary judgment motion(s) denied, case proceeds toward trial.
Other Pre-Trial Motions [Fed. R. Civ. Proc. 7(b)]	• Generally, any party can file a motion at any time to seek any form of relief from the court. • Parties seeking relief file a *motion*; parties answering the motion file a *response* or an *answer*. • Motion *in limine* — seeks instruction from court barring mention of particular evidence that is considered to be highly prejudicial to moving party.
Settlement/Status Conferences [Fed. R. Civ. Proc. 16]	• Generally ordered by court. • Matters for discussion: ○ Scheduling. ○ Informal dispute resolution; court may order mediation. ○ Delimiting issues/causes of action. ○ Other matters as dictated by the court or suggested by the parties.
Voir Dire [Fed. R. Civ. Proc. 47]	• Questioning/selection of prospective jurors. ○ Prospective jurors drawn randomly from adult citizens in a particular geographic area. ○ Some exclusions apply, which vary by jurisdiction. • Questioning may be by counsel or judge. ○ Generally by judge in federal court. • Possible challenges:

	○ For cause — specific and compelling reason to believe that a person cannot be fair or unbiased or is otherwise incapable of serving as a juror in a particular case.
	○ Peremptory challenge:
	  ■ Right of attorney to reject a certain (usually very small) number of jurors without stating a reason.
	  ■ Constitutional limits — cannot be based on gender, race, or national origin.

Trial [Fed. R. Civ. Proc. 38-53]	• Presentation of evidence to finder of fact.
	• Evidence presentation framed on either side by counsels' opening statements and closing arguments.
	• Evidence includes testimony, documentary evidence, and illustrative evidence.
	• Presentation of evidence:
	○ Presented first by plaintiff, then by defendant, with a rebuttal by plaintiff.
	○ Each witness subject to:
	  ■ Direct examination by the party sponsoring witness.
	  ■ Cross-examination by opposing party.
	  ■ Re-direct examination by party sponsoring the witness.
	  ■ Re-cross by the opposing party.
	• Decider of questions of fact:
	○ Jury.
	○ Judge in "bench trial" if right to jury trial waived.

Judgment as a Matter of Law [Fed. R. Civ. Proc. 50]	• How ordered: ○ Court *sua sponte*. ○ Court on the motion of a party made any time before the case is submitted to the jury. • Renewed motion may be made after judgment. • Standard: ○ A "reasonable jury would not have a legally sufficient evidentiary basis to find for the party on that issue."
Jury Charge [Fed. R. Civ. Proc. 51]	• Instructions by court to guide jury deliberations. ○ Provide guidance as to legal factors, burden of proof, damages, rules for deliberation, etc. • Often based on proposed instructions submitted by parties.
Verdict [Fed. R. Civ. Proc. 48, 49]	• Jury deliberates in private after submission of the case. • Jury decides facts and applies facts to the law as charged by the judge.

	• May be general or special verdict:
	  ○ General verdict — verdict that finds in favor of plaintiff or defendant and, if appropriate, the amount of damages.
	  ○ Special verdict — judge may order that jurors respond to specific written questions on issues of fact.

Stay of Judgment [Fed. R. Civ. Proc. 50]	• Judgment may be immediately enforceable upon entry (see below) or enforcement may be delayed depending on type of case and other circumstances.
Entry of Judgment [Fed. R. Civ. Proc. 58]	• By clerk of court. • Without or at court's direction, depending on the nature of the judgment.
Appeals [Fed. R. Civ. Proc. 77-80]	• Aggrieved party may seek appeal to higher-level court. • Appeals based on alleged error of law — appeals courts will not review factual issues. • Statutes and court rules govern the taking of appeals. • See Part C.

C. APPELLATE LITIGATION

This part addresses the following:

- Devices for Seeking Appellate or Supreme Court Review (1.)
- Federal Appellate Litigation Process (2.)
- Special Issues Involving Appellate Court Review of Agency Action (3.)

1. Devices for Seeking Court of Appeals or Supreme Court Review

Appeal	• Suggests *right* to take case to a higher level court.
	• From where taken:
	  ○ From U.S. district court to the court of appeals — matter of right.
	  ○ From U.S. district court to the U.S. Supreme Court when prescribed by statute (very rare).
	  ○ From U.S. court of appeals to the U.S. Supreme Court when prescribed by statute (very rare).
	• See Part C.2.

Petitions for Review	• Taken from federal agency to district court or court or appeals, depending on the agency's statutory provision on judicial review. • Parties:

	○ Petitioner(s) = party seeking review of agency decision.
	○ Respondent = agency whose decision is under review.
	○ Intervenor(s):
	■ Party to the underlying agency proceeding who has an interest in the appeal.
	■ Intervention may be on the side of the petitioner (supporting the outcome sought in the appeal) or the respondent (seeking to uphold the agency decision).
	• See Part C.3.
Petition for Writ of *Certiorari*	• Taken to the U.S. Supreme Court from:
	○ Federal court of appeals.
	○ State court of last resort, if decision based on question of federal law (statutory or constitutional).
	• Parties:
	○ Petitioner = party seeking review of lower court decision.
	○ Respondent = party defending lower court decision.
	• How Sought:
	○ Petition for a writ of *certiorari*
	○ Respondent files Brief in Opposition to Petition for a Writ of *Certiorari*
	• How Granted:
	○ Rule of Four = petition granted if four Justices vote to hear the case.
	○ Denial not accompanied by any statement of reason.

2.   Federal Appellate Litigation Process

Federal Rules of Appellate Procedure [Fed. R. App. Proc. or FRAP]	• Primary set of rules that govern appeals in federal court.
	• Consult and follow circuit court rules.
Notice of Appeal Fed. R. App. Proc. 3]	• Mechanism by which appealing/petitioning parties notify court and opposing party of intent to appeal lower court or agency determination.
Interventions [Fed. R. App. Proc. 15(d)]	• Process by which interested persons that are not direct parties in the appeal/review proceeding seek court order allowing their participation.
	• Normally, intervenors may not introduce into the proceedings issues not raised by the principal parties.

Docketing Statements/Other Court Filing Requirements [Fed. R. App. Proc. 12]	• Court requirements that parties submit information about the case, related cases, the parties' corporate affiliations, and other related information.
Motions [Fed. R. App. Proc. 27]	• Any party may file a request for relief of any type at any time in the proceeding.
Briefing Schedule [Fed. R. App. Proc. 28]	• Court-imposed briefing schedule. • Court may solicit suggestions from the parties.
Record [Fed. R. App. Proc. 10-11, 16-17]	• The record consists of the contents of the proceedings of the district court or the agency. • Includes all filings by all parties, all transcripts and other pieces of evidence, all court or agency pronouncements, and anything else that was before the court or agency in making its decision that is the subject of appellate court review. • The appellate court's review will be limited to the contents of the record.
Petitioner's/ Appellant's Opening Brief [Fed. R. App. Proc. 28(a)]	• Brief on the merits. • Attempts to show legal error in the disposition below and reasons why the lower court or agency determination should not be upheld.
Respondent's/ Appellee's Responsive Brief [Fed. R. App. Proc. 28(b)]	• Response to opening brief, arguing that lower court or agency decision should be affirmed.
Petitioner's/ Appellant's Reply Brief [Fed. R. App. Proc. 28(c)]	• Opportunity for petitioner/appellant to reply to arguments raised in respondent's/appellee's brief.
Oral Argument [Fed. R. App. Proc. 34]	• Responsive argument between petitioners/appellants and respondents/appellees. • Judges on panel typically interject questions for the litigants. • Court may decide case without oral argument on the merits of the briefs, based on panel decision that oral argument would not be necessary.
Decision/Entry of Judgment [Fed. R. App. Proc. 36]	• Court's decision will usually be issued some time after oral argument (this is taking the case "under advisement"). • On appeal, court will review issues of law *de novo*, and will independently conclude whether district court made the correct rulings.

Petition for Reconsideration/ Suggestion for Rehearing *En Banc* [Fed. R. App. Proc. 35, 40]	• Petition for Reconsideration asks the panel on the case to reconsider its ruling. • Suggestion for Rehearing *En Banc* is a request that the entire court sit together to consider the panel's determination. • Discretionary with the panel or court. • Rarely granted.
Mandate [Fed. R. App. Proc. 41]	• Mandate = formal order of the court. • Issues 21 days after an appellate court announces its decision in a case. • Issuance of the mandate will be delayed in the event of the filing of a petition for rehearing or a petition for a writ of *certiorari*.
Supreme Court Review [Part III and Part IV of the Rules of the Supreme Court]	• Parties may seek appeal to Supreme Court in limited cases. • Parties may seek discretionary Court review through a petition for a writ of *certiorari*.

3. Special Issues Involving Appellate Court Review of Agency Action

Threshold Issues	• Threshold issues of standing, finality, ripeness, and mootness may play a particularly significant role in these cases. • See Chapter 4.A.2.c.
Jurisdiction and Venue	• Consult Administrative Procedure Act and agency enabling legislation.
Special Rules of Procedure	• Title IV of the Federal Rules of Civil Procedure, Rules 15–20.

Deference	• Courts defer to agency interpretation of statutes which they are charged with administering.
	• Rationale for deference:
	  ○ Separation of powers.
	  ○ Expertise.
	• *Chevron* doctrine:
	  ○ Requires that a court uphold an agency construction of a statute it is charged with administering as long as the agency's construction of that statute is "reasonable" and not inconsistent with the language of the act.
	  ○ Two-step test:
	    ■ Does the statute have a plain meaning? If the statute has a plain meaning, that meaning will control its application.

	■ If the statute's meaning is not clear on its face, the agency's interpretation will be upheld if it is "reasonable."

D. COURT ISSUANCES AND DISPOSITIONS

This part addresses the following:

- Sources of Court Issuances (1.)
- Court Dispositions (2.)

1. Sources of Court Issuances

In addition to the sources listed below, many federal and state courts publish their opinions on the respective court website virtually simultaneously with issuance.

Slip Opinions	• Paper issuances provided to parties soon after issuance by court. • Limited copies may be available to the press and the public.
Advance Sheets	• Initial printed version of the court's reported opinion. • Paperback form, later incorporated into bound reporters.
Reporters	• Bound, final version of the reported court's opinion.

2. Court Dispositions

a. General Court Dispositions

Order	• Court resolution of a motion. • Court may grant a motion, deny a motion, or grant or deny a motion in part. • Includes "ordering paragraph" which sets out the court's judgment and any requirements imposed on the parties or lower tribunals. • Court may issue orders *sua sponte.*

Opinion	• Written document explaining decision and reasoning of the court.
	• Includes:
	  ○ Statement of relevant controlling authority.
	  ○ Court's application of law to facts.
	  ○ Explanation of underlying principles and reasoning governing court's decision.

Memorandum Orders/Opinions	• Short orders that contain only a brief explanation of the basis for the court's decision.

Judgment	• Narrow disposition of the case. • Generally found at end of opinion.
Holding	• That portion of the opinion that answers the legal question raised by the facts of the controversy before it.
Decision	• Less precise term that may refer to the judgment, opinion, or holding of the court.
Decree	• Obsolete term. • "Judgment" is currently used in lieu of "decree."

b.   Dispositions Peculiar to Trial Court Practice

Grant	Grant = order the relief requested in a motion.
Deny	Deny = refuse to order the relief requested in a motion.
Sustain	• Court agrees with an objection, typically to evidence a party seeks to introduce. • If an objection is sustained, the evidence will not be received and the witness will be instructed not to answer the question to which the objection was raised.
Overrule	• Court disagrees with an objection, typically to evidence a party seeks to introduce. • If an objection is overruled, the evidence will be received and the witness will be instructed to answer the question to which the objection was raised.
Curative Instruction or Limiting Instruction	• Instruction given to jury to mitigate the effect of tainted evidence or question. • Designed to avoid prejudice to party against whom the evidence or question would operate.

Injunction	• Court order requiring a person to cease or refrain from engaging in a specific action or activity.
	• When issued:
	  ○ Discretionary with court.
	  ○ If plaintiff's rights are found to have been violated, court balances:
	    ■ Irreparability of injuries; and
	    ■ Adequacy of monetary damages if an injunction were not granted.
	• Permanent injunction - issued as final judgment in a case after full merits review.
	• Temporary injunction:
	  ○ Issued early in lawsuit to maintain status quo.
	  ○ Types:
	    ■ Preliminary injunction:
	      √ Notice to non-moving party.

	√ Hearing on motion typically held.
	■ Temporary restraining order:
	    √ May be ordered without notice to non-moving party.
	    √ Typically ordered for short period of time.
	○ Moving party has the burden to show the need, including the immediate likelihood of irreparable harm in the absence of the injunction and likelihood of success on the merits.

Interlocutory Ruling	• Ruling which may be appealed in advance of termination of the proceeding. • Relatively few rulings are subject to interlocutory review under federal law and in many states.

Judgment as a Matter of Law	• Request by either party that the court grant a verdict in its favor, made at the end of trial.
	• Standard for granting:
	    ○ Judge may grant when the evidence is so strong in favor of the moving party that a reasonable jury could not find for the other party.
	    ○ Evidence must be considered in light most favorable to the non-moving party.
	• Also known as a directed verdict.
	• Rarely granted.

c.   Dispositions Peculiar to Appellate and Supreme Court Practice

Affirmance	• Decision to uphold the decision below (that is, of the lower court or agency decision on appeal).
Reversal	• Rejection of holding of lower court or agency order. • Often accompanied by remand and vacatur. See below.

Summary Disposition	• Streamlined approach to appeals upon request of party.
	• May be summary affirmance or summary reversal.
	• Not specifically contemplated by the Federal Rules of Appellate Procedure.
	• Standards:
	    ○ Moving party must be clearly entitled to merits decision in its favor.
	    ○ Case does not implicate a complicated legal question.
	    ○ Record must be sufficient to allow meaningful consideration of the issue(s) on appeal.
	    ○ Court may require showing of exigency.

	○ Grant of motion must be efficient and fair.
Remand	• Return of case to the lower court or agency for further factual findings or for other resolution consistent with appellate decision.
Vacatur	• Cancel or annul previous ruling — underlying decision is set aside and becomes void and without effect. • Usually accompanied by a remand.
Modify	• Court upholds lower tribunal's decision with one or more modifications.
Mandate	• Official manner by which court's opinion is issued and takes on the force and effect of law. • Order of court directing lower tribunal to take specific action or make specified disposition.
Memorandum Opinion	• Unanimous appellate opinion with succinct decision of the court. • Generally not published and thus without precedential value. • Usually issued only when the decision is based on a well-established legal principle. • Will typically be issued when summary disposition granted.
Opinion of the Court	• Opinion of the majority of the court.
Concurring Opinion	• Separate opinion agreeing with the court's holding, but either disagreeing with the court's rationale or adding a rationale. • Limited or no precedential impact.
Dissenting Opinion	• Separate opinion disagreeing with the court's holding. • Does not have precedential impact.
Plurality Opinion	• Opinion of a group of judges in which no single opinion received the support of a majority of the members of the court. • Plurality opinion is the opinion that received the support of more judges than did any of the other opinions. • Precedential impact not clear: ○ The narrowest analysis essential to the result derived from a combination of all concurring opinions; or ○ The concurring opinion offering the narrowest rationale; or ○ The parts of the concurring opinions that overlap.
Per Curiam Opinion	• "By the court" • Usually but not always a brief announcement of the disposition without a written opinion.

Opinion on Rehearing *en Banc*	• Opinion on review of initial merits panel at request of one or more parties to the case. • Rehearing is often requested but rarely granted.
Overrule	• Court in subsequent litigation changes earlier announced rule of law. • May be explicit or implicit.
Certiorari Granted	• Grant of discretionary review by the United States Supreme Court. • Not a decision on the merits; does not reverse or otherwise directly affect lower court judgment. • As a practical matter, may undermine strength of lower court ruling until the Supreme Court resolves issue.
Certiorari Denied	• Refusal of the United States Supreme Court to entertain discretionary review of lower court decision. • Not a decision on the merits; should not be construed as having any precedential effect.

Chapter 6

LEGAL WRITING AND CITATION FORM

This chapter covers the following:

- Some Notes on Good Legal Writing (A.)
- The Interoffice Memorandum of Law (B.)
- The Motion and Motion Practice (C.)
- Appellate Practice and the Appellate Brief (D.)
- Legal Citation Form (E.)

A. SOME NOTES ON GOOD LEGAL WRITING

The Golden Rule of Writing	• Say what you are going to say. • Say it. • Say what you said. • Stop writing.

Five Cs of Legal Writing	• Clear:
	  ○ Write in plain English.
	  ○ Avoid legal jargon.
	• Concise:
	  ○ Short sentences and paragraphs are best.
	  ○ Avoid unnecessary verbiage.
	• Convincing:
	  ○ Your writing must convince the reader that your analysis is correct.
	  ○ Anticipate and respond to any questions that the reader would have as she proceeds through your writing.
	• Complete:
	  ○ Do not skip steps in the analysis — take the reader from step A through step Z.
	  ○ Do not assume that the reader understands reasoning that seems obvious to you.
	  ○ Do not assume that the reader is familiar with the facts of the case.
	  ○ Check paragraph structure to ensure smooth flow.
	• Candid:
	  ○ Be honest or you will lose your credibility.

	• Back up everything you say — all facts and legal conclusions must be substantiated.
Style Matters	• Margins — use traditional margins, *e.g.*, 1" on top, bottom, and sides. • Pagination: ○ Number all pages after page 1. ○ Numbering on page 1 is optional. • Font: ○ Text — 12 point. ○ Footnotes — 10 point. • Spacing: ○ Text: ■ Double-spaced. ■ No additional spacing between paragraphs. ○ Footnotes — single-spaced. • Paragraphs: ○ Begin each paragraph with one tab. • Important Note: ○ Above all is subject to firm/supervisor preference and court rule or order.

B.   THE INTEROFFICE MEMORANDUM OF LAW

This part discusses the following relating to the interoffice memorandum of law:

- Introduction to the Interoffice Memorandum of Law (1.)
- Guidelines for Writing the Interoffice Memorandum of Law (2.)
- Template of an Interoffice Memorandum of Law (3.)

1.   Introduction to the Interoffice Memorandum of Law

Defined	• Document prepared by an attorney for another, usually more senior attorney, in the firm. • Provides an analysis of the legal implications associated with a specific event or course of action (taken or proposed). • Referred to as a "memo."
How Used	• Internal purposes; may also be read by the client. • Primary purposes: ○ Educate and inform the reader. ○ Help the reader formulate and evaluate strategic options. ○ Help the reader counsel the client as to a course of action, including a possible litigation strategy.

Hallmarks	• Objective/neutral/balanced — must be unbiased in its presentation of the facts and legal analysis.
	○ Must not distort the law or manipulate the facts to favor a pre-determined outcome.
	○ Must present the full range of possibilities based on an objective and thoughtful analysis of the law given the facts presented.
	○ If there are open questions as to the veracity of certain facts or the legal analysis, disclose them and present alternative analyses.

2.   Guidelines for Writing the Interoffice Memorandum of Law

a.   Format of the Interoffice Memorandum of Law

Follow Supervisor Instructions or Firm Template	• Some firms/attorneys have their own preferred format/template for the Interoffice Memorandum of Law.
	• Always follow personal style preferences of your organization or supervisor.
Components	• Typical components of an interoffice memorandum of law:
	○ Privileged and Confidential/Attorney Work Product legend
	○ Title of document
	○ Heading:
	▪ To:
	▪ From:
	▪ Date:
	▪ Re:
	○ Question[s] Presented
	○ Brief Answer[s]/Short Answer[s]
	○ Statement of Facts
	○ Legal Discussion
	○ Conclusion
	• See chart immediately below.

b.   Components of the Interoffice Memorandum of Law

Privileged and Confidential/Attorney Work Product Legend	• State verbatim on top right corner of memorandum.
	• Indicates for any future discovery that the document constitutes mental impression work product and is exempt from discovery. See Chapter 5.B.2.

Title of Document	• "Memorandum" or "Memorandum of Law" or "Interoffice Memorandum of Law." • Should be underlined and centered just after the privilege legend.

Heading	• Should be justified on the left margin, single-spaced, with a tab following each entry.
	• To:
	  ○ Refer to your supervising attorney by his or her full, formal name.
	  ○ Do not use titles such as "Mr.," "Ms.," or "Esquire."
	• From:
	  ○ Writer's full, formal name.
	  ○ Do not use titles such as "Mr.," "Ms.," or "Esquire."
	  ○ Initial final version to readily distinguish it from drafts.
	• Date:
	  ○ [Month] [day], [year] (*e.g.*, March 31, 2014).
	  ○ Do not use abbreviations.
	• Re:
	  ○ Give enough information to convey the client's name, and a short description of the subject matter of the memorandum.
	  ○ Include the case name and docket number if the matter is already in litigation.
	  ○ One or two lines, ideally.
	  ○ No need for full sentence — descriptive phrase sufficient.

Question[s] Presented	• Defines legal issue(s) that the memo addresses.
	• Format of heading:
	  ○ Heading should be centered on the document and underlined.
	• Direct or indirect question:
	  ○ Direct question: "Can . . . ," "Does . . . ," or "Is . . . ," for instance, followed by a question mark.
	  ○ Indirect question: "Whether . . . ," for instance, followed by a period.
	• Each Question Presented should be a single sentence.
	• Number of Question[s] Presented:
	  ○ One or multiple — each should address a different legal issue.
	    ■ One — no numeration
	    ■ Several — each should be numbered.
	  ○ May have sub-issues.
	• Concisely drafted to be read at a glance.

	• Should contain the following information: ○ Cause of action or issue. ○ Principal players. ○ Key relevant facts. ○ Jurisdiction whose law applies. • Objective — should not prejudge the outcome.
Brief Answer[s]/ Short Answer[s]	• Format: ○ Heading should be centered on the document and underlined. ○ Number of Brief Answers should mirror number of Questions Presented. • Begin with direct answer, *e.g.*, "Yes," "No," "Probably," or "Probably not." • The remainder of the Brief Answer should consist of one short, self-contained paragraph, which summarizes your conclusion and the reasons therefor. • Generally do not include citations, except when answer relies largely on statutory provision or case that establishes dispositive principle of law.
Statement of Facts	• Format: ○ Heading should be centered on the document and underlined. ○ May contain several paragraphs but generally should not be divided into sections. • Include any and all factual information that appears in the Legal Discussion. • Include only material facts, *i.e.*, those that are relevant to the legal analysis. • May begin with a brief summary of how the case came to you, who the client is, etc. • If the case is in litigation, include a brief statement of the procedural history of the litigation. • Narrative, chronological presentation usually works best. • Just the facts — no analysis. • Must be objective: ○ Present facts in a balanced fashion. ○ Do not promote favorable facts or minimize unfavorable facts. ○ Do not use words that are judgmental of actions taken by the client or others. ○ Note the source of facts. ○ Note any facts that are not known but would be helpful.

Legal Discussion	• Format of heading:
	  ○ Heading should be centered on the document and underlined.
	• Legal analysis — application of facts to the relevant law.
	• Remember your audience:
	  ○ Trained in the law.
	  ○ Not as knowledgeable as you in the details of the issue(s) or facts addressed in the memo.
	• Comprehensive:
	  ○ Fill in all gaps. Answer any question that the reader is likely to have as she reads the discussion.
	  ○ Should not presuppose any specific knowledge on the part of the reader.
	  ○ Make sure the reader has enough "raw material" to reach her own conclusions.
	• Pragmatic:
	  ○ Focus on legal issues presented in the context of the facts under consideration.
	  ○ Do not discuss merits of law or its historical development, unless directly relevant.
	  ○ Keep a practical orientation, with the goal of helping to guide the reader on a future course of action.
	• Use headings to guide the reader:
	  ○ Heading should correspond to Question[s] Presented and Brief Answer[s] and any sub-parts thereto.
	  ○ Numeration of headings:
	    ■ Major point headings should be preceded by a Roman numeral.
	    ■ The first level of sub-headings should be preceded by a capital letter.
	    ■ Further divisions should continue in standard outline format.
	  ○ Headings may be drafted in an objective, neutral fashion or in a way that reflects your conclusion.
	    ■ The latter is likely to be more helpful to the reader.
	  ○ Headings and sub-headings must be grammatically and stylistically internally consistent.
	  ○ Taken together, all headings should give the reader a complete picture of the legal issue(s) under consideration.
	• Objectivity is critical:

- ○ Recall goals of memo — to *educate and inform* the reader; to *predict the outcome* of a potential legal dispute; and to help the reader *evaluate various potential courses of action* to be able to effectively *counsel the client.*
- ○ Accordingly, the discussion should be balanced and objective and should not skew the law or the facts to reach the result desired by the client.
- ○ Discuss even negative precedent. See Chapter 4.B.6.
- Common organization — TRAC formulation for each issue and sub-issue:
  - ○ T = Thesis = Single statement of the issue and its predicted outcome (issue + conclusion, briefly stated).
  - ○ R = Rule = statement of applicable law (see below).
  - ○ A = Application = application of the facts presented to the established legal standard (see below).
  - ○ C = Conclusion = summary of conclusion of the analysis presented.

***

- Rule = the law:
  - ○ Applicable legal rules in relevant jurisdiction.
  - ○ Identify specific elements or factors of a given rule.
  - ○ Cite cases to support legal rules and to discuss specific elements or factors.
    - ■ Cases are proof of statements of legal principles.
  - ○ Stick to the law — do not mention or allude to facts.

***

- Application = application of facts of your case to the established law:
  - ○ Use headings and subheadings to the extent appropriate to your analysis.
  - ○ Each section and sub-section should begin with a thesis sentence that describes the issue being discussed and your conclusion with respect to that issue.
    - ■ Do not be concerned that the thesis statement is redundant of the heading.
  - ○ Your analysis should be guided by the facts of your case, analyzed under the applicable law.
  - ○ Call upon and cite precedent as may be necessary to support your analysis.

○ Include analogies to and distinctions from the facts presented and facts found in applicable precedent.
○ Discuss both strengths and weaknesses of conclusions you reach:
  ■ Discuss most likely outcome first.
  ■ Then discuss weaknesses of that conclusion and factors that might weigh in favor of another result.
○ Which cases to discuss?
  ■ Factually similar cases:
    √ Focus on cases that are more factually analogous to the case at hand.
    √ "Factually analogous" is not "factually identical." Allow yourself to be flexible enough to see factual similarities where they might not be immediately apparent.
  ■ Cases that exemplify legal doctrines — use cases, even if factually distinct, to the extent that they seem to explain, or modify important rules or doctrines or to the extent that they may be considered to be landmark cases in the jurisprudence on your issue.
  ■ Cases issued by higher-level courts:
    √ When selecting cases, remember the hierarchy of courts within your jurisdiction.
    √ Obviously, it is preferable to include more cases from higher courts than from lower courts.
    √ Lower court cases may at times be extremely important, and you should not shy away from using them when they provide added value.
  ■ More recent cases:
    √ All other things being equal, it is preferable to rely upon more recent cases than upon older cases.
    √ Of course, all other things are rarely, if ever, equal. You may find cases that have become landmarks in that they continue to be cited and relied upon frequently.
    √ There may also be old cases that are more factually relevant than newer cases and which you would not want to ignore in your legal analysis. Accordingly, do not discard old cases for that reason alone.

	√ A good way to show the court that a rather old case remains good law is to indicate that it has been cited or quoted with approval in a newer case.
	■ Cases from other jurisdictions — in the absence of relevant authority in your jurisdiction, it is appropriate to cite to opinions issued by other state courts or to federal court decisions which apply your state or some other state's law.
	○ Each section/sub-section should end with a conclusion as to what was just addressed.
	○ If you think that more facts would be necessary in order to reach a definitive conclusion or complete your legal analysis, indicate which facts would be important and how they might affect your analysis and conclusions.
	○ Footnotes should be used sparingly to raise points of interest that are not directly under analysis.
	○ Citations to authority:
	  ■ Citations should be in text of memo.
	  ■ Use proper citation form, including signals, pinpoint citations, and explanatory parentheticals as appropriate.
	  ■ See part E.

Conclusion	• Format of heading: ○ Heading should be centered on the document and underlined. • May contain several paragraphs but generally should not be divided into sections. • Summary of the legal analysis: ○ Greater detail than in Brief Answer[s] with some description of the reasons supporting the conclusions reached in your memorandum. ○ Include practical suggestions and recommendations. ○ Indicate issues that might still be researched but which are beyond the scope of the task. ○ Be as definitive as possible without misrepresenting the law or ignoring risks.

3. Template of an Interoffice Memorandum

PRIVILEGED AND CONFIDENTIAL
ATTORNEY WORK PRODUCT

MEMORANDUM

TO: [Supervisor's full, formal name; no titles]

FROM: [Your full, formal name; no titles; initial final version]

DATE: [Month day, year]

RE: [One phrase; include client, legal issue, a few material facts]

QUESTION[S] PRESENTED

[1.]   [Question[s] Presented should state the legal issue[s] addressed in the memo. The Questions Presented become in substance the major point headings for the Legal Discussion, *infra*.]

[2.]   [Number each Question Presented if more than one.]

BRIEF ANSWER[S]

[1.]   [There will be a Brief Answer for each Question Presented.]

[2.]   [Number each Brief Answer if more than one.]

STATEMENT OF FACTS

[Typically, there is no need for headings, formal sections, or numbered paragraphs. Use traditional paragraph format. A chronological narrative generally works best. Any fact alluded to in the Legal Discussion section must be included in the Statement of Facts.]

LEGAL DISCUSSION

[Use introductory text as may be appropriate.]

[I.] FIRST MAJOR POINT HEADING*

[Use introductory text as may be appropriate immediately after any point heading.]

     A.   Divide Major Issue Into Subsidiary Issues.*

         1.   Further divisions can be made.*

         2.   Break down your analysis as much as feasible.

     B.   Taken Together, Headings Should Give the Reader a Summary of Your Analysis.

---

* Note that Roman numerals are followed by capital letters, which are followed by Arabic numerals, followed by lower case letters, etc.

C.   Make Sure that Your Headings Are Internally Consistent.

    1.   Sub-headings must relate to the major point heading that precedes them.

    2.   All headings at the same level should be presented in the same style.

[II.] SECOND MAJOR POINT HEADING

[Use subheadings as above.]

CONCLUSION

[No headings, formal sections, or numbered paragraphs. Use traditional paragraph format.]

C.   THE MOTION AND MOTION PRACTICE

This part covers the following elements of the motion and motion practice:

- Introduction to Motion Practice (1.)
- Template of Motion (2.)
- Template of Memorandum of Points and Authorities in Support of Motion (3.)
- Template of Draft Order (4.)

1.   Introduction to Motion Practice

Defined	<ul><li>Motion = request for relief from court.</li><li>Various types, including:<ul><li>Fairly routine procedural matters (such as a request to extend a deadline); and</li><li>Highly controversial matters, including those that are dispositive on the merits (such as a motion to dismiss).</li></ul></li></ul>
Parties in Motion Practice	<ul><li>Any party may file a motion.</li><li>Movant/moving party = party filing the motion.</li><li>Respondent/non-moving party = party answering or responding to the motion.</li></ul>
Time for Filing	<ul><li>May be prescribed by rule or court order.</li></ul>
Goals	<ul><li>Educate — inform the court and your opponent about the merits of your position.</li><li>Persuade:<ul><li>The court — seek a favorable ruling from the court.</li><li>Your opponent — show strong hand in the hopes of exacting favorable settlement concessions.</li></ul></li></ul>
Common Types of Motions	<ul><li>See Chapter 5.B.2.</li></ul>

Components of Motion Filing	• Three components:
	  ○ Motion.
	  ○ Memorandum of points and authorities.
	  ○ Draft order.
	• Each of these components is discussed below.

Motion	• Short document.
	• Contains the following elements:
	  ○ Case caption.
	  ○ Identifies party seeking relief.
	  ○ Identifies relief sought.
	  ○ Refers to accompanying memorandum of points and authorities in support thereof.
	  ○ Indicates if motion has support of non-moving party.
	• See section 2.

Memorandum of Points and Authorities	• Memorandum of Points and Authorities in Support of Motion:
	  ○ Provides the legal analysis that justifies the granting of the motion.
	  ○ Party in opposition will file a Memorandum of Points and Authorities in Opposition to the Motion.
	  ○ Some practitioners loosely call these memoranda "briefs," although the term "brief" is more appropriately used in appellate practice.
	• See section 3.

Draft Order	• Draft of order moving party wants the court to issue.

2. Template of a Motion

[Complete case caption, including court and case number]

[PLAINTIFF XXX'S] MOTION FOR [RELIEF SOUGHT]

[Party designation] [party name] hereby moves this court for an order [state nature of the relief sought].

The grounds for this motion are set forth in the accompanying memorandum of points and authorities.

DATED: [city], [state] [date submitted]

Respectfully submitted,

[Counsel's name]
[Law firm name and address]
Attorneys for [party designation] [Party name]

3.   Template of a Memorandum of Points and Authorities in Support of Motion

[Complete case caption, including court and case number.]

[PLAINTIFF'S] MEMORANDUM OF LAW
IN SUPPORT
OF MOTION FOR [RELIEF SOUGHT]

[PRELIMINARY STATEMENT]

[1. In one short, self-contained paragraph, identify the parties (giving, within parentheses and in quotations, the shortened name you will use in the document to refer to each party, if relevant), the nature of the lawsuit, perhaps a *few* details about the case, the procedural posture, and the client's position on the motion [*e.g.*, supporting motion for summary judgment].]

[2. The preliminary statement must be short and concise. It should be a single paragraph, probably containing no more than two or three sentences. Its sole function is to help orient the court as to the nature of the pleading and the procedural context in which it was filed.]

[3. Use this opportunity to begin to educate the reader and develop the reader's sympathy for your position.]

[4. There should be no heading for this section; it should simply begin immediately following the caption and title of the pleading.]

STATEMENT OF FACTS

[1. The Statement of Facts should be *comprehensive*. It should contain all of the factual information necessary to support your legal argument. You may not in your Argument rely upon or refer to facts that were not presented in the Statement of Facts.]

[2. The Statement of Facts should be *persuasive*. This is the first real opportunity you have to persuade the judge of the propriety of the relief you are seeking. *Be an advocate.* Frame the facts in the way most favorable to your client.]

[3. The Statement of Facts should be *credible*. Every word in your Statement of Facts should beyond reproach. Do not be misleading. Do not distort the facts. Do not omit material facts that are necessary to present a complete picture of what happened. Indeed, the Statement of Facts is the perfect place to confront "unfortunate facts" in a way that allows you to neutralize them as much as possible.]

[4. The Statement of Facts should *tell a story*. A good Statement of Facts is not a dry recitation of facts, but a story punctuated with color. Do not simply dryly summarize the testimony of various witnesses. Instead, interweave testimony from various witnesses to shape the narrative and make your story compelling. Lead the reader toward your conclusion and imbue your Statement of Facts with a strong sense of the theory of your case. Upon reading the Statement of Facts, the judge should be ready to rule in your favor. Use this as a test for editing your work.]

[5.Give *just the facts*. Limit yourself to the facts, but use transitional words and phrases to shape the narrative and move the story along.]

[6. Do not be argumentative or appear to make conclusions in the Statement of Facts. Use artful word choices to set the right tone and suggest obvious inferences. Conversely, use more neutral language to diminish the impact of unfavorable facts.]

[7. Use thoughtful words when describing testimony. When referring to the testimony of your witnesses, words like "testified," "indicated," "noted," "observed," "confirmed," and "emphasized," to name a few, make good choices. When referring to the testimony of adverse witnesses, words like "suggested" and "contended" are good choices; when trying to undermine that testimony, words like "acknowledged," "admitted," and "conceded" make good choices. But avoid *ad hominem* attacks on witnesses and on your opponents.]

[8. Use a chronological approach and end the Statement of Facts with a *brief* description of procedural history.]

[9. Include citations to the record: The record refers to the original papers and exhibits filed with the court/agency as well as the transcript of any proceedings. There should be a reference to the record for every factual allegation made in the Statement of Facts (and, for that matter, in the Argument). Record citations should appear often in your Statement of Facts. Do not make the reader guess the source of your information; make it easy for the judge or clerk to find the place in the record where a fact to which you are citing can be found.]

[10. Use quotes from the record in the Statement of Facts. Be sure that your use of quotations from the record does not detract from the narrative, but instead flows naturally. Try to integrate quotes with your text.]

ARGUMENT

[1. The Argument section is the heart of the memorandum. It will provide the legal basis for a decision in your favor.]

[2.   Use headings and sub-headings to guide the analysis:

    a.   There should be a major point heading for each issue.

        i.   Each major point heading begins with a Roman numeral. If there is only one major point heading (*e.g.*, one issue) there is no numeration.

        ii.   Each major point heading contains a one-sentence statement of the basis for your legal argument.

        iii.   Each major point heading will be in all capital letters.

    b.   There should be sub-headings within the major point headings.

        i.   Sub-headings should be more specific and reflect sub-issues presented under each major point heading.

        ii.   Each sub-heading should be preceded by a capital letter followed by a period, and underlined. Use upper and lower case letters for the text of the sub-headings. Capitalize the first letter of each word in the sub-heading.

    iii.   Sub-headings, like major point headings, should state an affirmative proposition that you will prove in that section of the Argument.

  c.   Additional levels of sub-headings should be used to reflect further divisions of the sub-issues.]

[3. Taken together, the headings should provide a roadmap for your argument. Each major point should reflect a complete and independent basis for a ruling in your client's favor. Each sub-point should support that main heading. Headings should state the proposition and should contain, concisely, enough facts and law to indicate why your thesis is correct.]

[4. All headings (including sub-headings) are to be underlined, end with a period, and should be single-spaced when longer than one line.]

[5. If portions of your argument go to the entire issue presented by a major point heading, include it before you get to the sub-headings.]

[6. If the same legal issue applies to more than one major point heading, the appropriate place to set forth the general parameters of that issue may be before *any* of the major point headings. The main goal in this respect is to state the law or an issue in a place where, as a matter of logic and organization, it will be seen as applicable to those sections that follow it.]

[7. Procedural matters common to motions practice are familiar to the court. Accordingly, there is no need to overdo a discussion of the law in those areas. The resolution of most motions is likely to be fact-specific, so placing particular emphasis on the facts is usually a much better expenditure of the writer's time and space.]

[8. The following elements are critical in preparing an analysis for a memorandum of law in support of or opposition to a motion:

  a.   Major point heading — The major point heading should represent the issue presented.

  b.   Thesis sentence or paragraph — A thesis sentence or short paragraph should follow the major point heading and essentially restate the major point heading. That is, it should present the issue to be addressed and the desired outcome.

  c.   Analysis — An analysis of the law presented in light of the facts of your case. Include a discussion of why any seemingly contrary authority does not control the outcome here.

  d.   Each section will end with a conclusion restating what you have just shown.]

[9. Fact-intensive — The Argument will be very fact-centered and may contain very little legal discussion or analysis. Use record citations to support your facts.]

CONCLUSION

[Different attorneys take different approaches to the Conclusion. Alternatives include the following:

- Summarize the substance of the argument just presented.
- Simply state "For the foregoing reasons" *or* "Accordingly [party on whose behalf the brief is filed] respectively requests that the Court [provide the requested relief]." If you need to elaborate, chances are your legal argument is not clear or cogent enough.]

> DATED:City, State [date submitted]
>
> Respectfully submitted,
>
> [Your name, firm name, and address]
> Attorney for [name of party]

4. Template of Draft Order

[Complete case caption, including court and case number.]

ORDER

Upon consideration of the motion of [party filing motion] for [nature of relief sought] and the opposition thereto, this Court hereby ORDERS that the motion be granted and [describe the relief sought].

ENTERED this _____ day of _____, 20 _____.

> _____
> [Name of Judge]
> [Title, *e.g.*, United States District Court Judge]

D. APPELLATE PRACTICE AND THE APPELLATE BRIEF

This Part discusses the following relating to appellate practice and the appellate brief:

- Notes on Appellate Practice (1.)
- Components of an Appellate Brief (2.)
- Template of an Appellate Brief (3.)

1. Notes on Appellate Practice

Appeal Defined	• Formal request by a party dissatisfied with a judgment of a lower court or agency that a higher court review the decision below.
Right to Appeal	• Right of appeal to intermediate appellate court in many cases. • Some cases may require permission to appeal, *e.g.*, interlocutory appeals.
Starting an Appeal	• File Notice of Appeal, if required by court rule.

Parties to an Appeal	• Appellant or Petitioner = party taking appeal. • Appellee or Respondent = party opposing appeal and supporting the decision below. • State practice may vary.
Judges in an Appeal	• Panel of odd number of judges generally presides.

Interlocutory versus Final Decisions	• Interlocutory decisions:
	  ○ Orders at an intermediate stage in ongoing proceeding.
	  ○ Can deal with a range of legal issues that may arise during a case — everything from decisions on scheduling to evidentiary matters and motions to dismiss.
	  ○ In federal court and some states, appeals generally not permitted of interlocutory decisions.
	• Final decisions:
	  ○ Appealable.
	  ○ A decision is final when it ends the action in the court in which it was brought, leaving nothing more to be decided.

Review of Legal Issues Only	• Appeals limited to questions of law.
	• Factual questions generally not appealable.
	• No new facts may be presented on appeal:
	  ○ Appellate review limited to record established below.
	  ○ No jury on appeal.

Review Limited to Record Below	• Issues on appeal must have been raised at the trial court level. • Parties are not permitted to raise legal objections for the first time on appeal: ○ The trial judge must first be given the opportunity to rule on questions of possible error.

Briefs and Oral Argument	• Brief = written argument to the appellate court demonstrating why the lower tribunal's determination was incorrect and should be reversed or was correct and should be affirmed.
	  ○ Opening brief:
	    ■ Filed by appellant/petitioner.
	    ■ "Topside" brief.
	  ○ Responsive brief:
	    ■ Filed by appellee/respondent.
	    ■ "Bottomside" brief.
	  ○ Reply brief = filed by appellant in response to arguments made in responsive brief:
	    ■ Optional, but most parties file them.
	    ■ Concise: should be as short as possible.

	• ■ Function: should be limited to responding to arguments raised by adversary.
	• Oral Argument:
	○ Sometimes but not always ordered by the appellate court.
	○ Opportunity for each side to present arguments in its favor and for the judges/justices to ask questions of the attorneys that can help them resolve any doubts that they may have about the case.
Appellate Court Determinations	• The appellate court may affirm, modify, reverse, or remand the lower tribunal determination.
	• Affirm = no reversible error found; lower court/agency decision is left intact.
	• Modify = lower court/agency decision modified in some way.
	• Reverse = reversible error found and lower court/ agency decision typically vacated and remanded.
	○ Vacate = cancel/annul the lower court/agency determination.
	○ Remand = case sent back to the lower tribunal for further action consistent with appellate court decision.
	• See Chapter 5.D.
Standards of Review	• Defined:
	○ Level of deference an appellate court gives to the rulings of the lower court whose decision is under review.
	○ Appropriate level of deference is determined by the issue under review (see below).
	• Applicable standards of review:
	○ Clear error/clearly erroneous:
	■ Applies to findings of fact.
	■ Highly deferential to lower court.
	○ *De novo* review:
	■ Review "from the beginning," with no deference to lower court.
	■ Applies to questions of law.
	○ Abuse of discretion:
	■ Applies to issues within the discretion of the trial court/agency.
	■ Question is whether the trial court abused its power, even if the appellate court would not have reached the same conclusion itself.

Court Rules	• Locate, read, and follow applicable rules.
	• Rules relate to format, content, and deadlines for filing briefs.
	   ○ Supreme Court:
	     ■ Rules of the Supreme Court of the United States
	     ■ Supplement with *Supreme Court Practice* by Robert L. Stern, Eugene Gressman, Stephen M. Shapiro, and Kenneth S. Geller (also known as "Stern and Gressman")
	   ○ Courts of Appeals:
	     ■ Federal:
	       √ Federal Rules of Appellate Procedure (FRAP).
	       √ Local circuit rules.
	     ■ State:
	       √ Rules of relevant state appellate court, when in state court.

2.   Components of an Appellate Brief

Overview	• Rules typically provide for the following contents of an appellate brief:
	   ○ Cover Page with Caption.
	   ○ Table of Contents.
	   ○ Table of Authorities.
	   ○ Statement Concerning Jurisdiction.
	   ○ Question[s] Presented.
	   ○ Statement of the Case.
	   ○ Summary of the Argument.
	   ○ Argument.
	   ○ Conclusion.
	   ○ Signature block.
	   ○ Joint Appendix.

Cover Page with Caption	• Court name, preceded by the words "IN THE." • Party names, separated by a v., on the left margin • Docket number to the right of the names of the parties. • APPEAL FROM, followed by the name of the court/agency from which appeal is taken. • Name of brief (*e.g.*, APPELLANT'S OPENING BRIEF, BRIEF OF RESPONDENT, APPELLANT'S REPLY BRIEF)

Table of Contents	• Contains every heading in the brief with the corresponding page reference. • Argument point headings, taken together, should offer a compelling outline of the Argument.
Table of Authorities	• List each constitutional, statutory, regulatory, judicial, and other authority cited in the brief. • Different types of authorities are grouped together under corresponding headings. • List authorities alphabetically or numerically within each category. • Each authority has page number(s) corresponding to where it is referenced in the brief.
Statement Concerning Jurisdiction	• Statutory basis for the court's jurisdiction, with relevant citations.

Question[s] Presented	• May be called Question[s] Presented, Issue[s] Presented, or Statement of Issue[s].
	• Components:
	  ○ Statement of the legal question before the court.
	  ○ Sufficient reference to material facts of the case to make the statement of the question concrete.
	  ○ Reference to the governing law.
	  ○ Brief introductory statement may be included when it would aid in the understanding of the question presented.
	• Number of Questions Presented:
	  ○ One for each separate legal issue.
	• Format:
	  ○ Generally presented in the form of a question, beginning with "Is," "Does," or "Whether."
	• Characteristics:
	  ○ Should be clear, concise, and comprehensible.
	  ○ Take on the role of an advocate but do so in a way that preserves your credibility and is not overly argumentative or defensive.

Statement of the Case	• Two components:
	  ○ Procedural history.
	  ○ Statement of the facts.
	• Procedural History:
	  ○ What has happened in the case thus far?
	• Statement of Facts:
	  ○ Limit to facts in record below.
	  ○ Characteristics:
	    ■ Accurate — never misrepresent facts.
	    ■ Complete — cover all material facts relevant to your argument.

	■ Compelling — the facts should be subtly persuasive. ■ Legislative facts — relevant statutes and cases and other sources — may be included.
Summary of Argument	• Required by some court rules and not by others. • Usually a good idea to include one unless: ○ Proscribed by rule; or ○ The case is extremely simple. • Write it after you write the argument itself. • Generally to follow same structure as the Argument. • Synopsis of the most important parts of the Argument: ○ Middle ground between Question[s] Presented and Argument.
Argument	• Heart of the appellate brief. • Present strongest arguments first, unless there are strategic or other reasons not to. • Organization of argument section of the brief: ○ Separate section with point heading for each Legal Question. ○ Each section should begin with a paragraph that summarizes the argument as to that issue. ○ Subsections can be used to discuss elements or factors associated with the issue under discussion. ○ Within each section or subsection, present your strongest point and argument first; then respond to weaknesses in your argument. ○ At the end of each section or sub-section, summarize what you have just demonstrated. • Use of point headings in argument: ○ Each argument section and sub-section should begin with an adversarial point heading. ○ Each heading should reflect an independent and complete ground for ruling in your favor as to that particular point. ○ Format of headings: ■ Conventional outline format. Starting with Roman number I; subheadings start with A, etc. ○ Functions of headings: ■ Cogent organization of argument. ■ Allow reader to navigate and select sections s/he is interested in reading; taken together, they present a comprehensive and compelling story of why you win. • Use of precedent: ○ Brief citation to authority may be sufficient.

	○ Sometimes more complete discussion of relevant precedent may be needed. • Argument must contain a theory of the case: ○ Should comport to law/precedent; and ○ Offer strong policy/common sense justifications. • Use of statutory language: ○ Any relevant statutory language should generally be presented at the outset. • Style and tone: ○ Stylish, interesting writing can attract the attention of the reader. ○ Tone should always be respectful of the reviewing court and the court/agency whose decision is being reviewed. • Bottomside brief should: ○ Evaluate whether arguments raised on appeal were properly preserved below. ○ Generally rely on the legal conclusions made by the tribunal below but may undertake an alternative theory of the case.
Conclusion	• Short statement of the relief requested. • May also briefly summarize the grounds upon which the relief is sought.
Signature Block	• Name and address of attorney(s) and party represented. • Date of submission.
Joint Appendix	• Contains relevant portions of the record below including pleadings and judgment. • Prepared by parties jointly. • Begins with a table of contents. • References to the record in the appellate brief are made to pages in the Joint Appendix (JA).

3. Template of an Appellate Brief

A template of a typical appellate brief is set forth below. Readers are cautioned to review and follow all applicable court rules.

IN THE UNITED STATES COURT OF APPEALS FOR THE
[NUMBER/NAME OF CIRCUIT]

[Name of appellant], Appellant

v.   Case No.   [ ]

[Name of appellee], Appellee

APPEAL FROM THE UNITED STATES DISTRICT COURT FOR THE DISTRICT OF XXXX

[OPENING/REPLY BRIEF] OF [APPELLANT/APPELLEE] [NAME OF PARTY]

TABLE OF CONTENTS

- [Table of Contents should reflect all parts of the brief, with page numbers.]
- [Check your final pagination to ensure that the Table of Contents accurately reflects any last-minute changes to the brief itself.]

TABLE OF CASES AND AUTHORITIES

- [List of cases and other authorities cited in the brief.]
- [Cases are to be listed first, by jurisdiction, in alphabetical order.]
- [Other authorities should be listed after cases — constitutional provisions, statutes, regulatory sources, legislative history, secondary authorities, and other authorities, in that order.]
- [Add page numbers to reflect location in brief where each reference can be found. Use *passim* for references to authorities that appear often.]

STATEMENT CONCERNING JURISDICTION

- [Statement, supported by applicable citations, of the basis for jurisdiction in the district court or agency from which the appeal arose.]

QUESTION[S] PRESENTED

- [Issue[s] should be presented in adversarial but credible form.]

STATEMENT OF THE CASE

- [Procedural history and facts of the case.]
- [Facts should be fair and honest but should have an adversarial slant.]
- [Citations to the facts should be to the record or joint appendix.]

SUMMARY OF ARGUMENT

- [Summarize the salient points of the argument.]
- [Encapsulate the theory of the case.]

ARGUMENT

- [Heart of the brief.]
- [Ample use of headings and sub-headings for issues and sub-issues.]

CONCLUSION

- [Concise statement of the relief sought and the reasons therefor.]

DATED: City, State [date submitted]

Respectfully submitted,

[Your name, firm name, and address]
Attorney for Appellant [name of party]

E.   LEGAL CITATION FORM

This section covers the following:

- Introduction to Legal Citation Convention (1.)
- Who Sets Citation Norms (2.)
- Using the Citation Manuals, In General (3.)
- General Rules of Style (4.)
- How to Cite Authority (5.)
- How to Quote from Authority (6.)
- Case Citations (7.)

1.   Introduction to Legal Citation Convention

What is a Legal Citation	• "Address" at which the reader can locate a cited authority.
	 • Citations exist for all sources, legal and non-legal.
	 • Attributes of citation conventions:
	    ○ Provide extremely precise and detailed rules.
	      ■ Every character and every space begs a question.
	    ○ Provide useful information in briefest amount of space.

Importance of Proper Citation Form	• Identify the document to which the writer is referring.
	• Provide the reader with enough information to locate the document cited.
	• Indicate how the cited document supports the writer's point.
	• Provide the reader with important additional information about the cited authority, for instance, the year of issuance, the court issuing a judicial opinion, the author of an opinion or of a book or article.
	• Establish the writer's credibility; incorrect citations can:
	  ○ Be distracting to the reader; and
	  ○ Leave the reader with the impression that the writer is unprofessional and lacks attention to detail.

2. Who Sets Citation Norms

In General	• No national citation-setting authority.
Two Primary Citation Conventions	• *The Bluebook: A Uniform System of Citation.* • *ALWD Citation Manual: A Professional System of Citation*
The Bluebook	• Published by the *Columbia Law Review*, the *Harvard Law Review*, the *University of Pennsylvania Law Review*, and the *Yale Law Review.*
ALWD Citation Manual	• Published by the Association of Legal Writing Directors
Bluebook and *ALWD Citation Manual* Compared	• Highly consistent with each other. • Comparison charts found in ALWD manual and on various websites.
State Court Rules	• Some state court rules prescribe format of legal citations to be used in documents to be submitted to the courts. • Supplement other traditional legal citation norms, especially with respect to the citation of state materials (statutory, administrative, and judicial). • Influence citation practice for non-court documents in their respective jurisdictions.
The Role of Large Commercial Publishers	• Have their own citation practice that advance their own marketing agendas and brands. • Use caution — these may not be consistent with accepted practice.

3.   Using the Citation Manuals, In General

Introduction to Using the Citation Manuals	• Perplexing at first.
	• Easy to use once understood.
	• Goal:
	  ○ Master how to use the manuals.
	  ○ No need to master the rules themselves.
	• Contain tools and quick reference guides, templates, and/or appendices that enable the user to easily access the appropriate rules.
	• Demonstrate how rules differ for documents prepared for law practice and those written by academics.

Style and Formatting Conventions Covered in Citation Manuals	• Citation manuals contain rules that cover every aspect of citation form and style.
	• The comprehensiveness of the rules reflects the level of detail required when citing.
	• Style and format conventions cover the following elements, among others:
	  ○ Typeface.
	  ○ Abbreviations.
	  ○ Spacing.
	  ○ Numbers.
	  ○ Page, section, and paragraph designations.
	  ○ Footnotes and endnotes.
	  ○ Internal cross-references.
	  ○ Short citation forms.
	  ○ Citation placement.
	  ○ Introductory signals.
	  ○ Ordering of case authorities.
	  ○ Explanatory parentheticals.
	  ○ Quotations.
	  ○ Underlining and italicization.

Documents Covered by the Citation Manuals	• Citation rules cover specific citation format for the full range of sources, including the following:
	  ○ Cases.
	  ○ Constitutions.
	  ○ Statutory codes, session laws, and other legislative materials.
	  ○ Court rules.
	  ○ Ethics opinions.
	  ○ Jury instructions.
	  ○ Administrative and executive materials.
	  ○ Treaties and other international materials.
	  ○ Foreign legal sources.
	  ○ Books and treatises.

	o Periodicals. o Dictionaries. o Encyclopedias. o Restatements. o Model codes. o Uniform laws. o Sentencing guidelines. o Loose-leaf services. o Practitioner and court documents. o Speeches. o Video and audio programs. o Unpublished works and working papers. o Commercial databases. o Emails.

4. General Rules of Style

Jump/Pinpoint Citations	• Pages in cited source standing for specific proposition cited. • Always use when quoting language. • Use in almost all citations, even when not quoting language.
Citation Sentences/ Citation Clauses	• Sentences — citation sentences begin and end with a period and appear at the end of a sentence of text. • Clauses — citation clauses are set off by commas and appear somewhere in the middle of a sentence of text.
Introductory Signals	• Indicate the relationship between the authority cited and the proposition for which it is cited. • The closer the relationship between the cited authority and the proposition for which cited, the more direct a signal you will use. • No signal is to be used when quoting from authority.

Explanatory Parentheticals	• Used to indicate some detail about the proposition for which source is being cited.
	• When to use:
	  o Strongly recommended where an introductory signal has been used.
	  o May also indicate some important information about the decision (*e.g.*, plurality, *en banc*, dissent, on rehearing).
	• Explanatory parentheticals are included in separate parentheses after the parenthesis required as part of the formal case citation.

| Abbreviations | • Citation manuals contain tables of abbreviations to be used in legal citations. |

5. How to Cite to Authority

Cite Liberally	• Heightens persuasive value and credibility of analysis.

Avoid "String Citations	• "String citations = long lists of authorities standing for the same proposition.
	• Use case authority as follows:
	  ○ Recent cases.
	  ○ Issued by highest relevant judicial authorities.
	  ○ Can also include landmark case that established legal principle.

Cite Primary Authority Whenever Possible	• Cite to all relevant primary authority — constitutional provisions, statutes, regulations, and cases, in that order. • Citations to secondary authority are generally discouraged in legal memoranda and briefs. ○ If necessary to cite to secondary authority, use authority with high persuasive value. See Chapter 1.B.3.
Criteria for Selection of Authority to Which to Cite	• Legal issue. • Jurisdiction. • Court hierarchy. • Similar/analogous facts. • Cases that announce, refine, or explain important rules or doctrines. • Year of decision — more current cases normally desirable; older landmark cases also important to cite.

6. How to Quote from Authority

Quote Selectively	• Particular relevance to issue being analyzed. • Particularly interesting, compelling language.
Avoid Long "Block" Quotes	• Block quotes are those that contain 50 words or more. • Readers tend to gloss over them so use them only when of great importance. • Block quotes should be indented on both sides and single-spaced; do not use quotation marks. • The citation should appear outside the block quote, either before or after the quote, but in the regular text, *not* as part of the quote.

Integration of Quotes Most Desirable	• Integrate short quotes — preferably a few key words or phrases — with text. • Language should flow uninterrupted and grammatically between text and quote(s).

Form for Quotations	• Absolute precision is required when quoting language from a case or other source.
	  ○ Use brackets ([ ]) to indicate small omissions and changes from the actual language of the quoted source.
	  ○ Use " . . . " to indicate that you are omitting language from the original quote.
	  ○ Never omit language in a way that is arguably misleading.

7. Case Citations

The following are components of a typical case citation:

Case Name	• Name of plaintiff, appellant or petitioner.
	• "v." (which stands for versus).
	• Name of defendant, appellee, or respondent.
	• Use appropriate abbreviations for all case names.
	  ○ Lists of abbreviations found in citation manuals.
	  ○ For natural persons, only the last name is used.
	• Case name is italicized or underlined.
	• A comma follows the case name.

Case "Address"	• Most cases are published in a reporter. • The heart of the address of the case will be the recognized abbreviation for the reporter. • The volume number of the reporter precedes the recognized abbreviation of the reporter. • The page where the case begins follows the recognized abbreviation of the reporter.
Parenthetical Information	• Date — the year of decision. • Court — the court that issued the decision if not clear from the reporter.
Examples	• *Atkins v. Virginia*, 536 U.S. 304 (2002). • *United States v. Windsor*, 133 S. Ct. 2675 (2013). • *Hart v. Massanari*, 266 F.3d 1155 (9th Cir. 2001). • *Naked Cowboy v. Mars, Inc.*, 571 F. Supp. 2d 446 (S.D.N.Y. 2008).
Short Forms	• When a case is cited multiple times in the same document, use one of the accepted short forms after the initial citation. • *Id.* refers to the immediately preceding authority.

| | <ul><li>○ Use only when it is clear to which authority you are referring.</li><li>○ Convert citations to *id.* format only once you are nearing a final draft to avoid confusion.</li></ul>• *Supra* refers to earlier cited but not immediately preceding authority. |

INDEX

[References are to sections.]

A

ADMINISTRATIVE AND EXECUTIVE LAW
Agencies
    Actions and issuances . . . 3[B]
    Federal administrative law and . . . 3[A]
Code of Federal Regulations . . . 3[C]
Federal Register . . . 3[D]
Presidential documents . . . 3[E]

AGENCIES
Actions and issuances . . . 3[B]
Appellate court review of agency action, issues involving . . . 5[C][3]
Federal administrative law and . . . 3[A]

AMENDMENT
Generally . . . 1[A][3]
Process (article V) . . . 1[A][2][e]

APPEALS (See CIVIL LITIGATION AND APPEALS)

C

CITATION FORM, LEGAL (See LEGAL CITATION FORM)

CIVIL LITIGATION AND APPEALS
Generally . . . 5[B]
Appellate litigation
    Generally . . . 5[C]
    Agency action, issues involving appellate court review of . . . 5[C][3]
    Court of appeals or Supreme Court review, devices for seeking . . . 5[C][1]
    Federal appellate litigation process . . . 5[C][2]
    Supreme Court review, devices for seeking . . . 5[C][1]
Court dispositions
    Generally . . . 5[D]
    Appellate and Supreme Court practice, to . . . 5[D][2][c]
    General court dispositions . . . 5[D][2][a]
    Trial court practice, to . . . 5[D][2][b]
Court issuances, sources of . . . 5[D]; 5[D][1]
Federal civil litigation process, preliminary points relating to . . . 5[B][1]
Party designations and roles in
    Generally . . . 5[A]
    Supreme Court of the United Sates, at . . . 5[A][3]
    U.S. Court of Appeals, at . . . 5[A][2]
    U.S. District Court, at . . . 5[A][1]
Process, civil litigation . . . 5[B][2]

CODE OF FEDERAL REGULATIONS
Generally . . . 3[C]

CONSTITUTION OF THE UNITED STATES OF AMERICA
Generally . . . 1[A]
Amendment
    Generally . . . 1[A][3]
    Process (article V) . . . 1[A][2][e]
Articles
    Amendment process (article V) . . . 1[A][2][e]
    Executive branch (article II) . . . 1[A][2][b]
    Full faith and credit and privileges and immunities (article IV) . . . 1[A][2][d]
    Judicial branch (article III) . . . 1[A][2][c]
    Legislative branch (article I) . . . 1[A][2][a]
    Ratification (article VII) . . . 1[A][2][g]
    Supremacy of federal law (article VI) . . . 1[A][2][f]
Component parts . . . 1[A][1]
Executive branch (article II) . . . 1[A][2][b]
Federalism . . . 1[A][4][b]
Full faith and credit and privileges and immunities (article IV) . . . 1[A][2][d]
Governing principles of constitution . . . 1[A][4][a]
Government structure created by constitution
    Federalism . . . 1[A][4][b]
    Governing principles of constitution . . . 1[A][4][a]
    National government, relationship between and among branches of . . . 1[A][4][c]
    Powers and checks and balances, separation of . . . 1[A][4][c]
Judicial branch (article III) . . . 1[A][2][c]
Legislative branch (article I) . . . 1[A][2][a]
National government, relationship between and among branches of . . . 1[A][4][c]
Powers and checks and balances, separation of . . . 1[A][4][c]
Ratification (article VII) . . . 1[A][2][g]
Supremacy of federal law (article VI) . . . 1[A][2][f]

D

DOCUMENTS, PRESIDENTIAL
Generally . . . 3[E]

DRAFT ORDER
Template of . . . 6[C][4]

E

EXECUTIVE LAW (See ADMINISTRATIVE AND EXECUTIVE LAW)

F

FEDERAL ADMINISTRATIVE LAW
Agencies and . . . 3[A]

[References are to sections.]

U

W